Imprfct

Imprfct

(Healing The Brokenness)

Steven Davie

There are a few dedications I'd like to make. The first is to my amazing warrior priestess of a wife named Anneke. She has taught me so much about how to be with life and converted some of my stubborn views to a more open, gentle outlook (not an easy task with me). She truly is the best partner I could have wished for. She is stronger than she knows, and her words and actions help more people than she knows too.

Next are my parents, John and Pauline. They stood by me, even when I pushed our relationship to the brink of snapping in my younger years. They also took over much of the parenting of my son when I became a single dad aged nineteen and couldn't cope with life. I couldn't have wished for anything more.

My son Keerin, who has had his own struggles. At times, it even seemed like history was repeating with the similarities of my story and his life. He's overcome so much and is one of the most determined people I have ever met. All I can say is: choose what you want and you can have it, as the force is strong in this one.

Finally, the brothers and sisters I have met, who have inspired me with their wisdom, reflections and kindness, or for just being them.
In no particular order:
Mitch and Tim (you know why)
Alan Wilson from You Revolution @yourevolution2
Rory Lamont and Shannon Brown from Caim @welcometocaim

Michael Roberts
Jo McCoy from Blissness @theblissness
Matt Pink @better_life_guy
Andy Ramage @andyramageoffical
Chrystal Day
Kirsty from Sober Buzz @soberbuzzscotlandcic
David Miller from Mantra Menswork @mantramenswork

Contents

Introduction

'd like to thank you for choosing my book and I hope it is of some service to you. I'd like to start my introduction with a poem, so you can get to know me better.

This poem came to me when I was at a low point in my life, struggling after years of depression.

From the void
Came
The source
From the source
Came
My life
From my life
Came
My truth

The meaning of this is once nothing existed, then existence came into being, from that I came into being and through the struggle of life I will find my truth. The day after I wrote this, I vowed I would never let myself get this low again. I put on my boxing gloves and I fought for myself and my truth. It didn't happen overnight and there were many peaks and troughs.

In fact, I'm sure there will be many more ups and downs, as that's life. But I now know it's not what happens to you that matters, it's how you react. If life knocks you down, get the fuck up and go again! There is no stopping, only forward momentum – funnily enough, something I learned through years of stagnation and learning how to break free from it.

As a permanent reminder of this, I had my poem tattooed on my back, as a metaphorical statement that this low point was now behind me and should be remembered but not dwelt on.

Sorry for diving in deep so quickly but that's me, I'm a heart on my sleeve individual. Don't worry, I promise to make you laugh during this book too – well, I'll try to – it's not all depression and tattoos.

Why have I chosen to write a book?

There are two reasons. The first is the achievement of writing a book. You see, I'd always struggled with language at school, and it made me feel dumb. I'd be able to easily grasp the subject matter and could verbally communicate complex concepts well, but when it came to reading and writing, it was difficult. With reading and writing being a big part of the learning and examination process in every subject at school, I struggled.

I was ridiculed by my schoolmates for this struggle; you know what kids are like. The fallout from this was that I believed them; I thought I was stupid. I took this perceived view of "not-enough-ness" and added it to a very big pile of low self-worth adjectives I'd collected: failure, fat, ugly, dumb, the list went on.

When you have this outlook about yourself and couple it with drink, drugs and emotional distress, it's a recipe for a big pile of poo! And that's where I ended up in my late teens and early twenties.

So, that brings me to the second and most important reason for writing this book. If you feel you are not enough as you are, a failure, you can't go on living the way you are, suffer from depression and can't see a way out, if you want to change but don't know how or think that it's too late and you've royally fucked up your life, then I'm here to tell you I've done and felt all this too. I've come out of the other side, and so can you!

If even one person reading this book relates to it and it makes a difference in their life, then I'll be happy. I'm not a lifestyle guru, I don't have all the answers, I can only tell you what worked for me. If the things I've tried ring true, then great, if they don't, find whatever resonates with you and hopefully this book will help you do that. I'm just a Scottish guy from the outskirts of a rough council estate who's here to tell you that whatever this issue is, it's fixable and it's only you who can fix it, with a little help along the way.

The first part of the book deals with the journey of my life from my birth in 1973 right up to 2020.

In 1992, my life started to skid out of control and from 1996 my life started to slowly take an upward turn, with a few kicks up the arse from the universe to help me along my way. By 2017, I had all I ever wanted, but there was still brokenness inside me, a yearning for more. From 1992 to

2017 I tried to find that more in people, places, substances and things.

From 2020, things really got going for me on healing that brokenness. I started to find what I needed was inside of me, I'd searched the world and it was in me all this time. DOH!

It wasn't about getting rid of the brokenness, it was about understanding it, knowing it, accepting it when it arises, passing through it and coming out of the other side.

The second and third part of the book deals with changes I made from that point. I document the changes that had the greatest impact in improving my life and eventually finding out who I was. If you have brokenness inside you, no matter what, it can be fixed, you are the happiness you are searching for, you are your own healing and believe it or not, healing you will heal others.

If you're ready to hear about an *Imprfct* bloke and my journey to mend the relationship with my brokenness, whilst laughing at my squinted view of life, this is the book for you.

I also want to make this accountability statement: if I do manage to make a profit from publishing this book, then be reassured it will be put to good use.

I'm a dreamer of dreams and so is my soul brother Alan Wilson. Alan had a vision of setting up a non-profit charitable foundation called Enter. With the help of myself, Pamela Marie Docherty, Ross Geddes and Jordan, that is what we will be helping Alan achieve in 2023. Enter is here to get help for those who are not receiving the attention they need from our current care systems.

These are Alan's thoughts on this:

"Chronic mental health problems and high rates of suicide continue to blight communities in Scotland, with one in three Scots likely to experience mental health problems in any one year.

That means over two million people will likely experience difficulties with their mental health in 2023 – at a time when the current medical system has never been less equipped to support them with access to the right services.

Enter is about transforming access to support and the widespread introduction of natural healing modalities and community as the antidote to resolving Scotland's mental health epidemic.

In Switzerland, they created a programme called Exit, which allows people to choose to end their own life with dignity. In Scotland, we have created Enter, which is an invitation to those who feel they don't want to live anymore to start again and to be treated with love, kindness and dignity on their healing journey.

We have the vision of creating a community where donations are made to make natural treatments available to those who need them most but are not in a position to access them.

This programme will help people stuck financially or on long waiting lists to access support outside of the faltering medical system. The programme will connect people with powerful natural healing modalities and Scotland's top well-being practitioners to facilitate a transformation to their health and well-being."

So, there you have Alan's vision, and this is where I intend to direct the profits from my book.

I had a vision of setting up a charity one day. I had journalled about this in 2021 and now it's come true, just not in the way I expected. I thought it would be my charity, but after speaking to Alan and the others, I realise no one owns a charity, there is no *mine* here. We are all just contributors to a force of change that will better humanity.

It's always best to aim really really high because, if you just fall short, you will have achieved greatness anyway. We are aiming high and, if you are an expert in the field of holistic mental health or have a media presence that may be of service, then get in touch, my contact details are at the end of chapter 26.

I plan to use my skills to be in service of others, bringing more healing to my brothers and sisters of this world. I will do this by coaching others, reaching out to those who are struggling, helping shape projects like Enter and, ultimately, I want to set up a retreat where holistic therapies help people. How are we going to fund this all? I don't know, that's not up to me, the universe will take care of that. My part of the bargain is to live and act in alignment with these projects and have faith it will all work out the way it's supposed to.

This book is about me, but it's for you; if you've ever felt there must be more to life than this bullshit, I ask you to read on and enjoy.

Part 1

1973 to 2020

CHAPTER 1

The Early Years

1973 to 1976

I was born in a hospital in Leith on the 18th of April 1973. Leith was once a distinct area from Edinburgh but is now part of Scotland's capital. However, some Leithers will tell you otherwise and are fiercely adamant of their independence from the city. I was born in Leith, but my parents stayed in Musselburgh, which was originally a small fishing town on the outskirts of east Edinburgh.

I come from a working-class family. My mum worked part time in a dental surgery, and in later years she went on to be a successful area manager in the retail industry. My dad worked as a miner back then and had a few different occupations when I was growing up, finally ending up owning his own taxi.

Although I can't really remember him, my parents told me tales of the crazy dog we owned then called Roy. He hated police cars and would chase them down the street if he ever saw them. He was also partial to running through the back greens of the tenements, ripping all the clean washing off the washing lines. As you can imagine, that didn't go down well with the neighbours. Roy was finally given away due to his unruly behaviour. We also had a cat named Fluffy, named because she was a big ball of black and white fluff.

The clearest memory I can recall is being on the small beach by Musselburgh Harbour on a summer's day with my mum. My dad did join us later – perhaps he'd been working earlier – and he gave me a toy metal aeroplane that was painted pure white. We only stayed in Musselburgh for the first few years of my life, then we moved to another part of Edinburgh.

CHAPTER 2

Go West

1976 – 1981

Aged three, my family moved to an area of Edinburgh in the west of the city called Dalry. At that time, the area was surrounded by many breweries and the smell of them filled the streets. My dad was now working as a removal man and started driving taxis part time. My mum was working in retail as an assistant manager and stayed in the same line of business throughout her working life.

A story I tell from living in Dalry that a lot of people can't believe is we used to get our milk delivered by horse and cart; the big Clydesdale horses could be seen going up and down the tenement streets every day. I still can't quite believe it myself; it sounds like I was alive in the forties.

I attended Dalry Nursery, where I have a vague memory of watching Punch and Judy shows. I also recall throwing up one day in front of my whole class. The most vivid memory I have was of going into a mock phone box that they had in the classroom. I picked up the phone (obviously disconnected) and I started to speak to someone. I could hear them clear as day. When I handed my nursery nurse the phone, she told me that she couldn't hear anyone. When I insisted the call was from her mum, she looked unhappy and said her mum was with the angels, then shooed me away to play with something else. (I was a freaky wee kid!)

Aged five, I started at Orwell Primary School, which had been renamed from its original name of Normal Primary (I know, what an odd name for a school, right?). The school was a five-minute walk from my house, but you could climb a fence at the end of my garden and get into the school playground in thirty seconds. I often took that route when no one was looking.

This is where some of my first feelings of "not being enough as I was" crept in. As I said in the introduction, I struggled with language, both reading and writing, and things like dyslexia weren't really a talked about thing. To this day, I still wonder if I suffer from dyslexia, but I've lived with it all my life and I get by, so I don't see the point of finding out now aged almost fifty. I have a memory of having to read standing up in front of the class and when I muddled my words some of the kids laughed. The fear of speaking in front of people stayed with me, until I faced that fear in my professional life.

I also remember being taken up to the headteacher's office. Three of us, Mark, Kenny and I, had blown up a fan in the toilet. Well, it was Mark and I that did it, but we both blamed Kenny. He got the belt across his hands for it. Back then, it was normal for teachers to physically hit kids for doing wrong. Kenny, if you ever read this, I am sorry for sticking you in it when you did nothing wrong, I didn't know any better back then.

I need to say I was loved and spoiled by my parents. There are no tales of neglect or woe on that front. I got all the best toys and even had an Atari in 1978. If you don't know what that is, it's an early edition of the first home gaming machines. Like a PS5 but a lot slower and with awful graphics but groundbreaking at the time.

In 1980, we went on our first trip abroad. It wasn't any ordinary trip; we went to Disney World in Florida. How many kids from that era can say that?

One positive memory I have of my time at Orwell School was the jannie (the janitor) who taught me how to play chess and I became quite obsessed by the game when I was young. Another memory of the jannie was that he'd served in the army in India. During his time there, he'd learned how to do shadow puppetry, and he used to do little shows in the playground for all the kids. I wish I could remember his name, but it escapes me.

CHAPTER 3

New Schools

1982 – 1990

I n 1982, we moved back to the east side of the city where I went to Niddrie Mill School, which was a completely different vibe to Orwell. The school was named after the housing scheme that surrounded it. Niddrie was a massive council housing estate and, during the eighties, the buildings had fallen into a serious state of disrepair. There was a massive unemployment issue and, to top it all off, there was a bad heroin problem in the area.

As you can imagine, a lot of the kids from this area had a tough home life and were quite wild in their behaviour. Orwell had been a small, quiet and peaceful school, Niddrie Mill wasn't. It was a shock to the system but, looking back, it gave me the experience of interacting with folk from different backgrounds. I wasn't the worst student, but I wasn't the best. I was okay at sports but average at best. I just kept my head down, trying not to draw attention to myself. My first teacher (who shall remain nameless) was a bit of an angry head, who was always shouting at us, and

I lived in a state of constant fear of her. To be fair, some of the kids she had to teach were a bit unruly to say the least, so acting like a dragon was how she coped.

The headteacher was called Mr Greig and he had a catchphrase; when he'd shout at some kids, he'd say, "You're a fooooool, boy, nothing but a fooooool!" He always extenuated the *ooo* sound. As you can imagine, when he wasn't around, we used to mimic and mock him. Our name for him was boiled egg as it rhymes with Mr Greig – well, that and he was bald.

In my final year of primary school, I had a teacher called Mr Rocks, who was great. If we got our heads down all morning and learned the boring stuff, he would let us play sports in the afternoon. As an incentive, it worked a treat.

I started Portobello High School in 1985, which was a large sixties building with around a thousand students. My mum and uncle had attended the school in years gone by. My reading and writing issues seemed to get worse (or, more likely, the curriculum got harder). I was put in remedial classes for English, so let's just say it made me feel as if I was stupid and not worth anything. With high school kids, any weakness is pounced upon and that's what some of them did. So, people were telling me that I was dumb, and I believed that, it made me think: *why should I bother?* And I didn't.

Throughout my life, I've used my sense of humour to make folk laugh; I was the proverbial class clown. It made me feel good making people laugh and it obviously made them feel good too. I saw life differently to others. I was once told I had a squinted view of the world and I agree, I do – it's something I celebrate now. When I pointed out my squinted insights about life, people would laugh. I guess this is how I derived my sense of worth and acceptance from my peers back then; I certainly didn't get any from my time in the classroom.

I was a chubby, awkward kid and the "not-enough-ness" got worse. It didn't help that I stretched to six feet tall aged twelve. Back then, that was tall for that age, and it made me stick out even further. Due to this stretching in height, I earned the nickname Tiny, something I'm still fondly called by my long-term mates. I'd use my humour to curry favour with the cool kids and struggled my way through high school.

Like a lot of teenagers, this is where my first experience of alcohol entered my life, aged fifteen. I would meet up with my mates from school on Portobello High Street. We would go to a local shop which would sell underage kids bottles of cider and beer. We'd scrap together what cash we had, buy some booze and head down the prom to down it as quickly as we could. I would often get sent into the shop to buy the alcohol as I was the tallest of the group.

By the age of sixteen, I could easily get served in a bar as asking for ID was unheard of. It's hard to remember when I started to drink every weekend, but it must have been around this time.

As you've probably guessed, I didn't really like high school and I didn't apply myself at all, I only wanted to dick about and party at the weekends. I left school at sixteen to start an apprenticeship as an electrician. I attended college as part of the apprenticeship, and I loved it compared to school. I also had the incentive to pass my exams because, if I didn't pass, I didn't move on to the next year and didn't receive a pay rise.

At seventeen, I started to dabble in smoking weed. This would have been in 1990 and, at this time, the rave culture was starting to bloom in the UK. I had always loved electronic music, as my interest had been fuelled by listening to Geoff Young's Big Beat Show on Radio 1 and listening to the music from the acid house scene of the late eighties.

This is where getting off my head would be taken to another level.

CHAPTER 4

Put Your Hands in the Air

1991 – 1996

1 991 was a massive year for me. Not only was I fully immersed in rave culture with all the substance use that came with that, but I also became a father aged eighteen. The mother of my son was nineteen. Looking back, we were kids ourselves, and not mature enough to handle the responsibility of parenthood. Although the weekends were a party lifestyle, we were both working and, with the help of my parents, we bought our own flat in Portobello.

I had become aware of house music when I was around thirteen in 1986. It was a form of electronic music that burst out of Chicago and Detroit and spread across the world. House music morphed out of disco, although was distinct due to new technology-based instruments. Although the music has evolved and the terms used to describe it have changed, the kids of today are still going out partying to their form of house music to this day.

Around this time, I started going to Buster Brown's

under-eighteens nightclub in Edinburgh. The DJs played house music that had reached the UK charts, such as Farley Jackmaster Funk's "Love Can't Turn Around" and Steve 'Silk' Hurley's "Jack Your Body". Music has always meant more to me than lyrics when it comes to that art form. If you think about it, why does music convey movement? Why do sounds make me want to wiggle my arse? It's always baffled me.

Over the next couple of years, the acid house phenomenon hit the UK and kids across the country were going to parties in old buildings, quarries and beaches. I would go to these parties and dance all night drug-free to start with, then eventually started to dabble in acid and ecstasy. I even remember buying my first acid tab on Portobello High Street from a guy we shall call Tiff (those who know, know). It was a strawberry, which was one of the more popular blotter designs. Boy, the trips were strong that night.

It was around 1992 when I started to attend nightclubs – Soma, 9c, Rezerection and a club called Pure – where I would meet most of my lifelong friends. We'd dance every Friday night, go to afterparties, which were sometimes of epic size, and we'd eventually stop the craziness on Sunday night, sometimes even Monday night.

During these parties, drug-fuelled conversations would be had on such topics as life and consciousness, but most of the time we'd just speak complete bollocks. On one such night clubbing with my mates Kev and Casey, we had been invited back to a house party in Leith, Edinburgh. There was a house full of people spread across each room of the flat. Everybody was high as a kite and the beers and pills were flowing.

I was sitting in the hallway of the flat with my two mates. We had been talking away when I suddenly had a thought, which I blurted out. "Do you think French pigeons can understand Scottish pigeons?"

Kev paused with a sense of bafflement on his coupon (Scottish for face) and answered, "What, do you mean like a bilingual pigeon?"

"Yeah, if it had lived here for a while and had learned the lingo, would it coo in a Scottish dialect but with a French accent?" I replied.

Casey suggested that we try out an experiment. His suggestion: we should try to coo like a French pigeon trying to speak Scottish. We could then see if we could understand each other.

What a fucking brilliant idea that was!

So, picture the scene, three guys in their early twenties, sitting in a hallway of a flat in Leith, off their tits on drugs and alcohol, trying to coo in Scottish with a French accent.

We had been doing this for ten minutes when suddenly a door opened. A girl that Kev liked called Bridget walked out of the living room and straight into the cooing mess of the hallway.

"What the fuck are you three up to?" she asked.

We explained; it didn't seem to help much. She answered, "Oh right, I see." She gave a laugh of disapproval then headed for the kitchen to refill her drink.

"That's your chances fucked there, Kev," I said.

Kev, Casey and I all erupted into laughter as the insanity that had just come out of our mouths in the last ten minutes dawned on us.

Much to my surprise, years later, I read a newspaper article that said scientists had proved that birds have regional dialects. So, perhaps not a leap of faith to suggest they have international languages coo – sorry, I mean too! Please feel free to google it, I'm not making this up.

This wasn't a one off. A typical night at an afterparty could involve us talking about steam-powered televisions, underwater swimming pools and even undercover elephants.

We were quite a mixed bunch of people in both age, background, dress and outlook. I was one of the younger crew, always dressed smartly in expensive and sometimes tasteless couture. Others were ten or even twenty years older than me; it was a hotchpotch of people.

We had lawyers, dropouts, university professors, plumbers, crusty techno traveller types and a myriad of others in our merry band. Every summer, there would be free parties on the beaches of East Lothian. We'd turn up with a sound system and dance the weekend away. It was like a second generation of hippies who were the product of Thatcher's UK in the eighties. I'll not go down the Thatcher route of discussion, nothing good will come of it. Let's just say, it was a great time to be young and Thatcher turned us into a generation of open-minded "be as one" rebels.

Drug use was the norm, and everyone in their teens

and twenties was "on it" back then. My recreational drug use was never really an issue in my life, to start with, at least. Sometimes the drugs were free thanks to mother nature providing us with magic mushrooms. In October 1992, a few mates from Pure and I went out picking liberty cap mushrooms and these weren't for our pizzas – yip, these were for tripping our balls off. Magic mushrooms are plentiful around the rural surroundings of Edinburgh and took tripping to ninja level. This is where shit got real! They aren't called magic mushrooms for nothing; there's something about the altered state you fall into with these things that is other-worldly. It can't be a coincidence that people who eat these fungi frequently report that they can see and, more importantly, feel how all things are connected to each other. This connected phenomenon was something I experienced on more than one occasion whilst tripping. The trips would range from staying in this reality with things looking a bit squinty and colourful, to speaking to other-dimensional beings with messages for me or watching a rainbow-coloured phoenix fly through my mind.

During these experiences, or shortly after having them, striking synchronicities would happen. I'm not going to list them, as I'll save the mind fuckery for later, but let's just say I'd think, *Come on, that's not just a coincidence.* As the years passed, strange synchronicities continued to happen, and they would always become more frequent through times of psychological or spiritual growth.

In January 1993, the relationship with my son's

mother finally broke down. It had always been a rocky one, especially when alcohol was in the mix. This is when my life started a downward spiral that would last for some years. We broke up and she left the family home.

The original plan was that she'd leave to find a stable place to live and, once that happened, she'd come back for my son. A year later, she hadn't come back for him and, from my point of view, it seemed she was quite happy living the single life. She may have a different view, of course, but that's how I felt at the time. This break-up just added more fuel to the "I'm a failure" fire.

At this point, my parents decided to go for custody of my son on my behalf. For the next few years, a messy court battle ensued, and my parents did more of the parenting than me. I could not deal with the pain of the break-up; I was not the responsible father I wanted to be and the debt I put my parents in with legal costs of the custody battle made me feel angry and like a burden. I couldn't hold down a job due to my partying. I just buried my head in the sand with drink and drugs and ended up a depressed mess. I had gone from recreational use to using drink and drugs to block out the pain.

My parents won the court battle after my son's mum was found out to have lied in court. This is a brief synopsis of what went on, but believe me, it was very messy and very hurtful for all involved.

In 1994, the criminal justice bill was passed, which placed loads of restrictions of movement and public gatherings of twenty people or more. It was the government's reaction to the rave generation. It made large, free parties illegal and targeted our music by singling out in the law that the restrictions applied to "music which contained repetitive beats".

This was just a ruling generation scared of youth, it's the same old story; they placed into law as much disruption as they could to make us stop. It was a mindless act of social engineering. I've seen a lot more unacceptable behaviours at mainstream music festivals than I ever did at any rave – illegal or otherwise – mostly because of too much alcohol, but the government had no issue with these gatherings.

I still love and listen to techno to this day and, although it's changed, the scene is still there for the youth of today to enjoy. People slate the kids today standing there with their phones filming the DJ and slate the DJ with their sets on a pen drive. I say, just let them get on with having a good time and don't turn into that which you rebelled against, a non-understanding old fart.

1994 was also the beginning of the end of the party scene for me. I needed to leave, it wasn't fun anymore. To give you a flavour of what was going on in my life at that point, a good friend of mine almost died bringing loads of pills back from The Netherlands in condoms he'd swallowed. The condoms burst in his stomach, and I believe they had to bring him back to life a couple of times in hospital. When he finally did get out of hospital, he got a four-year jail sentence. Although I'd never done that sort of thing myself, I was no innocent. Another friend ended up in a wheelchair for life after crashing at high speed on a stolen high-powered motorbike. I was surrounded by chaos and I wanted out. It took a further two years for me to leave this scene and make the first steps towards changing my life.

I'd like to dedicate this chapter to all the clubbers from that time. I know I will forget some, but you know who you are: Mason, Chris H, Heather S, Ronnie B, Dave U, Graham U, Mark B, Woody, Geordie Scotty, Johnny K, Martin, Steven C, Cat, Wee Kristie, Duggy, Kirsty L, Mike A, Neil T, Neil M, Big Bri, Middle Bri, Wee Bri, Mark D, Maria F, Leo F, Gerry, Lorna, Gerry D, Loogie, Moogie, Max, Mad Paul, Ruth, Stewart, Heather, Mo, Esther and all the rest too.

CHAPTER 5

The First Steps to Healing

1996 – 2003

I n the summer of 1996, after four years of acting like a complete party animal and not dealing with the pain I had been feeling, I ended up in a mess. The drink and drugs weren't blocking out the pain anymore, there was no high, there was only anxiety, depression and an inability to function in normal society. I hadn't dealt with any of the feelings I had, I just added them to the pile and tried to block them out. I couldn't hold down a job for any length of time and I knew I had to change something; I had to sort my life out. I had a young son who needed a better version of the dad that was turning up and that was reason enough.

I wanted to take stock and start to find some level of happiness in my life. In 1996, I started the very very very long road to recovery. I had friends in Newcastle, England, and I moved there to get some head space. I originally stayed at a friend's parents' house until I found a place of my own after two weeks of looking. I got a job in a bar and that gave me enough money to get by. I knew this wouldn't be forever, I just needed some time to gather the energy. I only lived in Newcastle for a few months, but this gave me the space to sort a few things out in my head. I was, however, still drinking three to four times per week.

I came back to Edinburgh full of energy to sort my life out. I got myself a job as a postman with Royal Mail and moved into my own flat in Edinburgh, with my son staying at my parents. I loved my time working as a postie – I saw it as getting paid to keep fit and it was great craic. But Royal Mail had a big drinking culture and that didn't help me much.

I had made some big steps, but I was still struggling with depression. No matter how long I waited, it wouldn't lift. I went to the doctor in 1998 and was prescribed medication. I didn't want to rely on another drug but at this point I had no choice. On the one hand, the antidepressants did work, but on the other hand, I still hadn't dealt with the feelings inside.

In 2001, I was still working for Royal Mail. I was also back living in the Portobello flat that I had lived in with my son and his mother back in 1991. My grandfather passed away that year and, after my depression had become worse, I decide to leave Royal Mail, sell my flat and go travelling for a bit. I had always had the instinct to see other countries but, looking back, I was still trying to run away from myself, which is never going to work, is it? I bought a round-the-world ticket going to LA, Fiji, New Zealand, Australia and Thailand, and off I went.

CHAPTER 6

A Steady Job

2003

Travelling gave me some newfound confidence, although, at first, I was prone to the odd panic attack. I couldn't cope with all the organisation of travel, thinking I'd fuck it up. But I did it and was ready to give normal nine-to-five life a go again.

In 2003, I started a job in the civil service. I'd never worked in an office environment before, so I had my reservations whether this job was for me. It turns out it was because, as I type this, I'm still working for them some twenty years later.

There was still eight more years of struggle to go but a stable job was the order of the day. In 2003, even though things had perked up and I had a more stable life, my depression would not shake for weeks at a time.

My new employer offered that, after of a year of employment, you could take an unpaid career break of up to five years and they would keep your position open for you. I had come into a little money, so I planned to go to India for six months. I'm incredibly grateful for all the support I received from my employer in those early "finding my feet again" days. The managers and welfare staff were immense, and they even helped and supported me when my mental health broke down again. A little trip to India and then a job to come back to, what could possibly go wrong? Lots!

CHAPTER 7

India, the Awakening

2004

Before I get to India, I need to introduce you to the spirituality part of my life. I know this won't be everybody's cup of tea but it's part of me and if I didn't tell you about it then I'd be hiding a part of my life that got me to where I am today.

I believe life has consistently presented me with signals that things are about to change or even need to change for my well-being. Sometimes this can come before crises or major life events. The signals let me know I'm on the right life path or if I need a nudge in the right direction. These signals come in the form of premonitions or heightened synchronicities in my life.

There's also an empath side of me where I know and feel how others are feeling. I mean, I don't just understand how someone is feeling, I feel it. We all have this ability to some extent, just some more than others. I'm sure you've walked into a room where you can feel the tension even if nobody's saying or doing anything, you just pick up the vibe. I'm not expecting you to believe me and, to be honest, my beliefs don't require you to. (A little *Matrix* quote there.)

Ever since I was a young child, I have felt a connection to something over and above what we would all consider physical reality. I'm not saying I walk around shouting, "I see dead people!" I just had what I call "a knowing sense".

I first started to notice these knowings, synchronicities, cosmic alignments, call it what you will, when I was around seven. They would manifest in relation to numbers at first. What do I mean by that? One example I remember was watching a film at a young age. The scene was in a casino, the camera was focused on the roulette wheel, the croupier span the ball, a feeling came over me and I knew – I mean without a doubt, one million percent knew – which number it was going to land on. It was seventeen, and yes, it did land on that very number.

I know I had a thirty-seven-to-one chance of being correct (for a UK roulette wheel). I totally understand the viewpoint that I just guessed it, as the feeling of knowing is only subjective to me. I can't make you feel what I feel, so I really have no way of proving it to you. I can only tell you what happens during these "knowings". If you don't believe me that's okay, but if you think about it, truthfully all you can say is you don't know, as you're not me, after all.

Others might say, "Well, if you really could do this then why aren't you a millionaire?" The simple answer is, I don't know when this is going to happen. I can't control it to make it happen. If it were a one-off event, I may have put it down to mere "coincidence" (not a term I believe in), but the frequency and the fact they still happen to this day makes me believe otherwise.

This sense developed further in my adult life where I would sense death or births with people who are close to me and, in fact, I still do. I remember telling a girlfriend from London who was living in my hometown of Edinburgh at the time that she was going to fall pregnant in the not-too-distant future with a baby boy. I went on to say that the baby wouldn't be mine, but I would be there when she found out she was pregnant. We split up not long after – can't imagine why! Yeah, I know, I should have kept that to myself.

Fast-forward two years to 1998 and my ex had moved back to London. I was flying back to that city from the opening game of the FIFA World Cup in France. We had remained friends, although I hadn't seen her since we'd split up. I had arranged to stay at hers for a few days and made my way to her flat. When I arrived, there she was with a pregnancy test! You guessed it, she was pregnant (not mine), and it turned out to be a boy. All this information came to me in a dream where I spoke to a ball of white light. Yeah, I know, freaky hippy nonsense, but there we have it, that's what happened. I've also had knowings where family members or friends were about to die or become seriously ill; as you can imagine, these aren't pleasant to deal with.

I've always had quite a deeply developed sense of empathy with people. I can feel what they are feeling as if it were my own feelings or thoughts. It's even stronger with people I know well. I've told a few people in my life about this but, until now, I've largely kept it to myself through fear of ridicule. I may be wrong, but if I had gone around my school and the building sites of the late eighties/early nineties when I worked as an electrician talking about this, I would have been eaten alive. I mean, I got nailed to the floor through my overalls whilst working on a building site on my eighteenth birthday! This was seen as a rite of passage; can you imagine me talking about this openly?

Even now, writing this down, I'm leaving myself open to ridicule. I'm sending this out into the ether without any idea of the repercussions. I know what I know and, if people don't believe me, think I'm crazy, or whatever, then fair play, that's their reality. People's opinions are merely that, an opinion – don't live your life by what other people think.

So, from an early age, I've always been aware there was more to life than stuff I could see out of the window.

Where were we again? Oh yeah, India in 2004. I left for India, which would throw up some crazy synchronicities and life-threatening encounters. India is a place you either love or hate, and I love it. To me, at least, for all its faults, it does have what I can only describe as a spiritual feeling about it. It's a place full of contrast; wealth and a LOT of poverty. You see beautiful temples and kids living under motorway overpasses. You smell amazing cooking fragrances and mountains of waste, and even death.

It's certainly not the easiest place to travel by road and train. When travelling by car in the city, there are no rules as such. The traffic feels like part of a giant organism flowing in one general direction, bumping into various other organisms going in different directions. When you get out of the city, the roads are a combination of *Wacky Races* and *Mario Kart*, you are never that far away from slipping on a banana skin and being catapulted off the road. As for the trains, they can range from being quite sedate to the downright crazy – that's when or *if* they turn up.

When I arrived in India for the first time in 2004, there weren't as many budget airlines as there are now, when there are multiple flights per day between the major cities. You can buy train tickets outside India nowadays, but you couldn't in 2004. A Google Translate app would also have been handy for navigating the Indian railways website, it's like a maze made of words with no sentences. After speaking to locals, though, this was the case for them too.

My first destination in 2004 was Mumbai and I spent a few days there sightseeing, eventually travelling south by train. I hopped on and off trains, staying a couple of days in each place, before finally reaching Palolem Beach in Goa.

When travelling to Palolem, I took the sleeper train and met two young English girls who were on their gap year. The train had open cabins of four bunks, and this was their first time travelling on their own. I could tell they were freaked out by the hustle and bustle of the train. We shared a cabin on the overnight journey, and they seemed a bit reassured by male company from the UK.

We were all heading to Palolem, so when we got off the train at Canacona, we shared a taxi to the beach. The beach is just over 1.5km long, has a typical palm tree look and has an array of beach huts, restaurants and bars. We arrived just before sunset and found basic huts for the royal sum of £2 per night. I got my head down for some sleep and was blissfully unaware of the crazy times that were about to unfold.

When I awoke, I went for a run along the beach. It was around twenty-six degrees at 7am and it would reach the low thirties every day. I sourced some breakfast at one of the many makeshift restaurants on the beach. Each year, they build restaurants for the start of the season in October, only to pull them all down again in May before the monsoons arrived. I had scrambled eggs on toast with lemon, honey and ginger tea. This became my routine most mornings. That first morning, I bumped into a crowd of people from South Queensferry, which is a place just outside Edinburgh. We talked for a bit, and I found out that an Australian girl Carmen who was travelling with them used to stay across the road from the old flat I had sold to start my travelling; she had lived there for three years at the same time as I had, although I had never seen her before. Synchronicity? Meh, nah, I didn't think so, just one of those things.

I spent my days drinking and socialising and I bumped into the gap year girls again. They told me they had met a Welsh guy called Will who I would have to meet. I asked them why and they said, "He's like you! Funny, always talking shit and joking." As I've said, I'd always been a bit of clown. I now know it stems from the people pleaser side of me, an adaptation to help me "fit in" and be part of the tribe. This adaptation comes from a feeling of being "not enough", something I wrongly coded my brain with through young life experiences. There are very few people who genuinely don't like to fit in. Some say they don't like to be part of a crowd, although I believe most of the people who say this do so to portray themselves as some sort of "rebel without a cause" type character. However, this goes against our primal instinct of belonging (if you're on your own in the savannah, a lion's gonna get you!).

I met Will and, sure enough, the guy was larger than life; the laughs we had were immense. I remember a time we convinced this girl from New Zealand that we were speaking Gaelic, which is a language spoken in Scotland and Ireland (although different versions in each country). The thing was, we weren't speaking Gaelic, we were speaking English quickly with exaggerated accents – we both knew what we were saying, but she didn't!

My £2 a night beach hut was great, it had all I needed – a bed, fan and one power socket – but I decided to move to the upmarket establishment where Will was staying. The place was called Cozy Neuk, and I think the huts were something like £10 a night, so we are not talking a five-star establishment, but it was a lot more luxurious than my original hut.

Being in India brought forward a creative side. I would scribble and draw and started designing T-shirts, mostly with slogans on them. I would take these designs to a local tailor to have them embroidered and started wearing them around the beach. A few people made enquiries about them, asking where I had bought them, so I told them

I'd designed them myself. It started off with one person asking me to design them a T-shirt, then another, then another. I would only charge them cost price as I enjoyed personalising them for people. On the neckline were the embroidered words "Mad in Edinburgh". I told people this was the brand name as a joke.

As the nights went on, the crowd of people grew. There were folk from England, Sweden, Australia, Italy and Denmark, to name a few. The drinks round the campfire each night were some of the best nights I've spent speaking to people on my travels. There was a new arrival to the beach that would spark a whole load of synchronicities and that's when the maddest incident-packed few weeks of my life would happen.

CHAPTER 8

The Guy Next Door

It was in my second week on the beach that the synchronicities started with the arrival of a new person.

As you can imagine, when you don't have to go to work, have no bills to pay and are a beach bum, you have quite a bit of time on your hands. I passed my time reading, talking, playing chess, designing T-shirts and learned to play a new game called Carrom.

Carrom is played on a large slate board. Each player has their own counters, which look like the ones you use when playing draughts. You flick the counters with your fingers and the aim is to get them in the holes situated at the corners of the board. That's the general principle of the game, but it's best to watch a YouTube video to get a better feel for it.

I played with the locals who were experts at this game. I remember them laughing at my rookie mistakes, but it was just a bit of fun. It was during one of these games when a new arrival at Cozy Neuk appeared. He was older than me, had a scruffy beard and greying hair. The owner showed him to the hut next to mine. He went into it and returned to sit on his porch around thirty minutes later.

I decided to go over to introduce myself. "Hello, I'm Steve."

He replied, "Pleased to meet you, I'm Graham."

I recognised the accent; he was also a Scotsman. This is the norm when you're backpacking, everybody speaks to everyone. It's not like a package holiday where you get to a hotel and stick to yourself bar speaking to one or two strangers.

I asked if he wanted a drink. I had found a new tipple in Honeybee, which is an Indian brandy. Graham replied, "That would be great," and I retrieved my bottle of hooch from my hut.

Graham told me he was from Dumfries and Galloway, but his accent certainly wasn't from there. It turned out he was from Edinburgh. A few more drinks went down, and he told me he grew up in an area of Edinburgh called Niddrie. I asked him his age and he said he was fifty.

"That's odd," I said, "my dad is fifty, and he grew up in the same place." After further discussions, I found out he went to the same school, stayed on the same street and he even had the same job as a teenager as my dad, delivering milk to the local households. I told Graham my dad's name, but he didn't recall him.

This was too much to be mere coincidence, though, I could feel it. It was the first of many synchronicities, but what was the lesson? We had a few more drinks and I left to go out for the evening with my crowd of reprobates.

I had arranged to meet them at our normal hangout for food, Cool Breeze. On my way there, I called home; I did this when I was away just to let my folks know I was okay. I told my dad about the chance encounter and, of course, asked him if he remembered Graham; he didn't recall him. However, there was enough connected randomness to say the meeting had meaning.

After another drunken night out at Cool Breeze, I woke up around 8am, dragged myself out of bed and went for a run along the beach. I got to the southern end and started to feel ill; hardly surprising given that I was doing exercise after a night on the tiles. I decided to walk back but began to feel faint. I noticed a crow had flown down just in front of me and was cawing like they do. There are hundreds of crows on Palolem Beach and they make some racket in the morning. Every time I walked towards it, it would fly just out of reach and caw some more. By this point, I was really struggling to stay upright. I just concentrated on the crow and kept walking. I shit you not, this not only continued for the full 1.5km of my journey back along the beach but also up the path that led off the beach right up to the door of my hut. The crow flew off when I stumbled in the front door to collapse in a heap on my bed.

I awoke around five hours later, thankfully felt much better and I decided to go out for some food. I noticed Graham was sitting smoking a cigarette on his porch again. I went over to speak to him, and thought, *should I mention what happened with the crow? I mean, he'll think I'm a nut job, won't he?* I plucked up the courage and told him the story.

I remember his words: "The crow is your spirit animal, it was looking after you, you should look out for them." It wasn't what I had expected him to say but I took it on board. We went on to discuss that I had always liked birds since I was a child and my favourite was a peregrine falcon. Guess what? Graham worked as a falconer in Dumfries, and he showed me pictures of the birds he trained, one of which was a peregrine. I found out that he came to Palolem to escape the Scottish winters every year; a lot of people do this from various parts of the world.

That night, I decided to have a night off the sauce, I went to bed early, and I awoke around 9am to those damn crows cawing like mad. I made my way out of the hut, looked up and there were hundreds of them sitting on the roof of my hut and no other hut but mine. I noticed Graham with his backpack at the reception desk – well, a wooden table disguised as a reception desk – it looked like he was checking out. He pointed to the crows on my roof and said, "You need to watch yourself, young man, they are trying to warn you of something." I didn't know it at the time, but he was right.

With that parting gift, he picked up his bag and he was gone. I never saw him again.

After Graham's bombshell of "they are trying to warn you of something", my first thoughts were of my family and friends – was something going to happen to them, was someone going to fall ill? I had a huge sense of dread and knew something was wrong; it was stronger than I'd ever had before. I didn't for a minute think about myself, but I should have. From that day on, I had a feeling of disease, something wasn't right. I called home, and everybody was fine. I tried to put it to the back of my mind, but it was always there.

A few days after Graham's departure, I was walking along the beach and noticed a couple sunbathing in my line of sight. As I got closer, I noticed that the female had a badge on her top; it was a Pure badge, the nightclub I used to go to in Edinburgh.

I stopped and asked, "So, are you a Pure-ist?" (The name that was given to attendees of the club.) She replied yes and we got talking. Their names were Michele and Stephen and it turned out, although we had never met, we knew loads of the same people. This is hardly surprising as we both came from Edinburgh, liked the same music scene, and went to the same nightclub. I invited them to join my crowd of friends later for one of the nightly bonfires we held. They came along to the bonfire and, from what I can remember, Will was on top form and it was another giggle fest of epic proportions. Michele and I crossed paths again back home some nine years later and she recalled it to be one of the funniest nights of her life.

Now, the reason I bumped into Michele again was I ended up marrying a close friend of hers called Anneke. As it turned out, Anneke was living in Michele's house the time of Michele's and my chance encounter on Palolem Beach. Anneke also grew up in Dumfries and Galloway, the same place as Graham.

Yip, I bumped into a girl on a beach almost 5000

miles from home, who had a flatmate at that time, then separately met said flatmate online and married her thirteen years later. We also recently came across a postcard that Michele had sent to Anneke from Vietnam on the same trip, postmarked on my birthday. That's synchronicity and quantum entanglement right there all rolled up into one.

Not enough for you? Here's some more synchronicities between Anneke and me.

In 2016, I happened to be on Anneke's sister Katie's Facebook page writing a comment on a photo when I noticed a guy I knew called C was one of her friends; this was someone I knew from the Edinburgh club scene of the late eighties and early nineties. I wondered how they knew each other. I asked Anneke, "How does your sister know this guy?" and found out it was a guy her sister Jacqui had known from her time in Edinburgh. I should explain Anneke and her family stayed in Lockerbie in Dumfries and Galloway until 1988 when they moved to Bedfordshire. Jacqui moved to Edinburgh in 1987 to go to university. C used to be up at my uncle's flat a lot around that time. I asked what time period that would have been, and Anneke told me it was the late eighties up to the early nineties.

I replied, "That's strange, he's a friend of my uncle's and C used to be up at my uncle's flat a lot around that time." In fact, he used to run nightclubs I attended. I may have even met Anneke's sister some twenty-two years before I met Anneke. My uncle now lives in Australia and, when I asked him, he did have a vague memory of Jacqui.

It doesn't end there. Anneke proceeded to tell me that

her sister used to stay in a flat at Potter Row, a student area of Edinburgh. At that time, she worked in a pizza shop on George the IV Bridge, which is just around the corner. This pizza shop was jointly owned by the mother of my son and her new partner, a place I often visited to pick my son up from after his mum had her access visit. Now, that's a fair bit of entangled-spanglement[1] spanning twenty-two years, many people and several chance meetings separated by thousands of miles.

And there's more! In future years, I found out that my boss had gone to school with Jacqui. If we were all living in the same city, fair enough, but Edinburgh and Dumfries and Galloway are eighty miles apart and Edinburgh and Bedfordshire are almost 400 miles apart.

When the synchronicity is this strong, I believe life is saying pay attention, this is important, and it was – these meetings were meant to be.

Okay, back to India. I stayed in Palolem for three or four weeks before I decided to move on. My original plan was to go north to Nepal but, like a lot of plans when you're travelling, it changed.

Will and I decided we were going to go to Sri Lanka together. We chose to get the sleeper train down to

---

1   My definition: "This is where individuals' life paths cross and connect at various points in their life, giving meaning to the connections. A lot of the time the people involved are not even aware of these connections." It is my dumbed down version of quantum mechanics and the unified field, where all things are connected, no matter which point of the universe they reside.

Thiruvananthapuram on the southern tip of India, and from there we would get a flight to Colombo in Sri Lanka. This is where my first life or death situation would happen.

We said our goodbyes to the friends in Palolem, telling them we'd be back in a few weeks, and we were off on the next part of the adventure.

CHAPTER 9

Let's Go to Sri Lanka

Will and I booked a train from Canacona to Thiruvananthapuram on some God forsaken class of ticket. As it was night when we got on board, it was pitch dark. The train had minimal lighting and people were sleeping on their bunks. The problem was, we couldn't find our bunks and they were all taken anyway. The train was packed – there were chickens in boxes flapping about and all sorts of craziness going on.

We decided to sit on the floor between the carriages and wait for the conductor to help us. I placed a sarong on the floor and sat down. I felt something run over my hand and pulled out a torch I had in my bag. The floor was crawling with bugs and cockroaches. I jumped to my feet after screaming like a five-year-old. Sometime later, the conductor turned up, we showed him our tickets and he took us to our bunks. He told the two guys who were currently occupying them to get off and we hopped on.

A brief time after that, an elderly man approached us, begging for money. He pulled back the top part of his robe to show a tumour the size of a head on his stomach. We gave him a few hundred rupees and he left. This is par for the course in India; you get people begging who are in a bad way or have a story to tell about their hardship. This isn't a dismissive comment, just an indication of the hardship some people find themselves in over there. Coming across such characters also depends on which cabin class you choose to travel in, as you don't get this in first class, that's for sure. My view is that it's easy to shield yourself from this and travel first class, but when backpacking I always found it fun to travel as cheaply as you could or, as I called it, the chaos class ticket.

Next up on "the madness train" was a guy selling rubber hammers that lit up and squeaked when you squeezed them. We passed on that sale. Then came the call of "CHAI CHAI" from the tea sellers. Next were the samosa sellers, and so on, just relentless chaos. All this was happening as the locals were staring at us wondering why these westerners had bought this class of ticket. I must admit, at points I questioned my thinking of *it will be fun to experience the local class of travelling.*

The journey was fourteen hours long, so after a couple of hours, I'd had enough of the chaos train experience and I decided to get some sleep as it was past midnight. I jumped up on my bunk and said to Will, "Fuck being awake for more of this shit, I'm taking some Valium." I had bought some for the journey from over the counter at the local pharmacy. For those who don't know, it's tranquilliser to aid sleep and anxiety. Will didn't want any, so I popped a couple and dozed off.

I awoke some eight hours later and looked down from my bunk. There was Will, eyes popping out of his head, which came about due to a combination of insomnia, mental torture of being asked if he wanted to buy a rubber hammer every twenty minutes, people speaking loudly, babies crying, chickens flapping about and the tea seller still shouting "CHAI CHAI"!

I remember his words to this day: "Ah, Rip Van Winkel, you're fucking awake! Now stay awake, as I feel like I'm losing my mind with this lot."

I couldn't help but laugh, I found it so funny. I got down from my bunk and distracted Will from the madness with some conversation. We eventually arrived in Thiruvananthapuram, got a place to stay for a night and flew to Sri Lanka the next day.

CHAPTER 10

Sri Lanka –
Colombo to Hikkaduwa

(No, not the detective, the city)

We arrived in Sri Lanka's capital city Colombo on the 4th of November, 2004. I had planned to travel down the west coast, round the south coast, do a few trips to the centre of the country and then travel back up the same route. At the time, there were areas in the north you were recommended not to go to due to the Tamil Tigers' civil war that was going on. My plan was to stay in Sri Lanka for Christmas and fly back to India for New Year.

We stayed a couple of nights in Colombo and booked a taxi to travel down to Hikkaduwa, which is a beach resort popular with surfers. When we arrived in Hikkaduwa, the weather was grey and overcast. It wasn't cold, by any means, but it wasn't as sunny as Palolem.

We met a couple of Swiss girls, Susannah and Daniela, and a guy from Manchester who was there for the surfing – his name escapes me now, so let's just call him Jack. The lazy days continued and, barring my runs in the morning, the most I did was read a book.

One morning, I decided to go for a swim in the sea. Will and the others were not around, as they were having breakfast. I went in for a dip and I wasn't that far out from shore. After around ten minutes, I decided to go back in, but no matter how much I tried, I could not get back to shore. At first, panic set in. I looked around, but there was no one on the beach as it was early.

I was caught in what is known as a rip current, which is where a channel of water is flowing against the waves and heads away from the shore. You are swimming towards shore but are not making any progress. This leads to exhaustion and, if you don't know how to get out of it, death! Luckily, I had passed my open water PADI diving course a few years before when travelling round the world. The advice came back to me: float, don't expend energy, swim parallel to the shore, as you will eventually get past the currents, and lastly wait for the waves to come to use them to propel you further in.

I set this guidance into action, but I was beginning to tire, and I felt myself going under. My life didn't flash before my eyes, but I did have the sense of "fuck this, I'm going out fighting". Thoughts of my son, family and friends came into my head and I started kicking my legs like mad back to the surface. I broke through, felt the air, took a deep breath and kicked like mad as the next big wave came to shore.

I put my feet down and I could feel the sand of the

bottom; I'd made it back to shore, but I was exhausted. I felt that I couldn't have carried on much longer. Adrenalin was racing through my veins, and I felt as light as a helium balloon. I headed back to my room, had a cold shower and collapsed on my bed.

This must have been what the crows were warning me of…? But it wasn't, there was more to come.

I told the others what had happened when I met them. I don't think they grasped the seriousness of the situation, I just got "ah man, that was a lucky miss" type of answer. The feeling of "something bad is going to happen" was still there, getting stronger. We stayed in Hikkaduwa for a few more days and then Will, Jack and I all travelled down south to Unawatuna.

CHAPTER 11

Unawatuna

(Put your hands in the air)

Unawatuna is a lovely place and one of the top ten beaches in the world according to some poll I read. The place was more set up for people staying at resorts and the prices certainly were a bit costlier for a backpacker's budget. We eventually found a place to stay at a reasonable price. We also found a small bakery where we'd knock on the door at 4am to get hot bread rolls stuffed with veg or fish whilst staggering home from our drunken escapades. (I loved those rolls!)

On the 14th of November, Will and I were getting ready to go out for some food and drinks. We were sharing a room to keep costs down and Jack was in another room. We had a balcony with a sliding door, which was open. From nowhere, a crow flew in through the open window and started to go crazy, flapping about the room.

It was like something out of a comedy movie, Will screaming "WTF is going on?!" whilst chasing this crow around the room, trying to catch it. I grabbed a towel from the bathroom and eventually managed to throw it over the crow. I picked up the towel with the bird still going bonkers and released it from the balcony. I looked at Will and, joking, said, "That's an omen, Will, something isn't right."

My thoughts turned to Graham's words still ringing in my ears: "You need to watch yourself, young man, they are trying to warn you of something." How right he was.

We called in for Jack and off we went for our nightly round of beers. We had some food and drink and I had decided to head back early, the other two wanting to stay out. I went home, fell asleep and woke up several hours later. Will still wasn't back and I thought, *That's odd, all the bars will be closed by now, I wonder where he is?* I got up and went downstairs to see if I could find him, just in case something had happened. I reached the bottom of the stairs and a group of around five or six men grabbed and overpowered me. They forced me to the ground, one put a machete to my throat and asked me for my wallet. I had around thirty US dollars on me, and I gave them it, I wasn't going to argue over thirty bucks. I started to struggle and a small handgun was pointed at my head. At this point, I thought fuck it, I'll need to just let this go where it's going.

They tied my hands and moved me to a quiet area where, low and behold, Will, Jack and the elderly security guard were all tied up. They asked for the room key, which I gave them. Although it was dark, I could tell the three of them had all been roughed up. They tied my legs with rope and proceeded to go upstairs and ransack our room. None of us had much money and they were obviously not happy about that; after about twenty minutes, the robbers came back down the stairs and whacked me over the head with the gun. They pointed the gun at my face again and said, "Where's your money?"

I've not told many people about this, but those I have always said, "You must have been shitting it." It's weird, I just remember feeling calm with a gun pressed against my head. I'm not trying to be macho or anything and I can't explain it, something was telling me I'd be okay.

I explained that we didn't have any and that we were not rich tourists but backpackers, so we didn't carry much cash with us. Again, I got another pistol whipping. I told them, "You can hit me all you want, I don't have any more money."

I think they put two and two together and eventually got that we didn't have any more cash. It must have dawned on them they were robbing the poorest foreigners in the vicinity, after noticing the backpacks in the room. That, coupled with the fact that even though I had a gun pointed at me, I wasn't giving up any more money.

I assume they decided to cut their losses and leave. They told us not to move for an hour and somebody would watch us to make sure we didn't. They could have been lying but we weren't going to take that risk. I say we – Will and I weren't. Jack decided to go for help after ten minutes and found out they weren't bluffing. Two guys appeared from the darkness as he walked down the path looking for help, grabbed him and proceeded to cut his face with the machete… and then they were gone, into the darkness.

The next few moments are hazy and hectic. We needed to get help for Jack and waiting about for an hour wasn't an option. Thoughts of the robbers coming back and us ending up like Jack went out of the window, it was time to act. I hopped down the path as my legs were still tied, hopping over the road to the next hotel to raise the alarm. When I got there, I asked the hotel receptionist to call the police. They seemed more bothered about what their residents might think than helping me. I don't remember how long it took for the police to arrive or where Will and Jack were, in fact Will may have even come with me to the hotel, it was just a blur.

We packed our stuff up from our trashed hotel room, jumped in the back of a police car and we were all taken to the local cop shop. Jack was patched up; luckily the cut wasn't that deep. We gave our accounts of what happened. It seemed like it was just a hassle for the police. I suppose life is different there and we were just three dumb tourists who could afford to be robbed.

So, this must have been the danger I was being warned of by the crows… but it wasn't!

We spent an age in the police station. When I was speaking to the police officers, there was a guy near to me handcuffed to a radiator; God knows what he'd done, but there was blood running down his face and he was either sleeping or unconscious.

I don't know how long we were in the police station, it

seemed like hours, but when we left, the three of us ended up arguing outside. Well, I should say, I started arguing with Jack. I went mad at Jack's actions trying to raise the alarm too early and the consequences we could have all faced. I think it was just a release of the shock of it all that made me react that way.

Will and I got the hell out of Dodge and Jack went his own way. We travelled back to Colombo in a taxi to chill and form a plan for our next moves. I don't think we said a word the whole journey; I just sat there thinking of the worst-case scenarios.

After two days in Colombo, we decided to go back to Palolem to spend a few days there. I decided I was going to go home for Christmas as I still felt on edge, and something still wasn't right. We got an email from Jack around the same time to say sorry, but to be honest, by this time, there was no judgement or blame, it was just the stress of the situation that made us all lose our tempers.

Now, the more eagle-eyed of you will have noted the year. Yip, 2004, the year the tsunami hit and killed 30,000+ people in Sri Lanka. It's a bit of an odd one that getting tied up and robbed at gunpoint turned out to be a massive stroke of luck. If this hadn't happened, then I would have still been in Sri Lanka when the tsunami hit. Given my plans at the time, I would have been on the return phase of my trip and would have been staying in one of the southern coastal resorts no more than fifty metres from the shoreline when the waves came.

I may have survived, I may not have, but on the 26th of

December 2004 the south and eastern coastal areas were devastated, and this is where most of the deaths were. My chances of survival would have been slim; I'm just thankful I got out in time.

I now know that this is why I was feeling so uneasy, as the danger was so great. Although I obviously didn't know this at the time, Graham was right, the crows were trying to warn me, so was the near drowning and the robbery; the universe was saying, "GET THE FUCK OUT OF THERE!"

The lesson from the universe here was: life can be taken away in an instant, so don't waste it. It was time to push on again, shed a skin and move to the next phase of life.

To this day, I still get warnings from crows. I've had two separate "crow incidents" this year (2023), only for a family member to pass the next day.

One of them was a bunch of crows landing on my roof and going crazy; one crow flew down and was banging against a closed window and flying in front of it, like it was trying to grab our attention.

I said to my wife Anneke that I knew this meant that someone would pass. The next day, my uncle passed. A similar thing happened the day before my step-gran passed.

I had told Anneke about my crow visitations in India and, not that I need a witness for validation, this was now proof as she saw this happen.

CHAPTER 12

The Return Home

During the robbery, my bank cards had been taken. Will kindly paid for everything until I had a chance to get a new card sent over and I could pay him back the money I'd borrowed. I had set up a joint bank account with my dad before I left on my travels in case I lost my card. I had intended to get my dad to send me his card over in the post and gave him a call to post it to me.

After flying back to India, Will and I took a first-class carriage back to Goa, no chickens or hammer sellers for us this time, and as for my travelling as locals do, that got chucked right in the bin.

On the train, we met two older men. It turned out one of them was a writer and the other a photographer. We spoke mostly to the writer. I thought his name was Kris Krishanderan and his book was called something like *A Little Bird*, but I have searched online to try and find a copy and haven't been successful, so perhaps I got his name wrong. Maybe he'll read this one day and I'll finally get a copy.

We discussed the robbery and Kris was interested in our story, which we told him. He then told us about his book, which was set in his younger days when he was a drug smuggler to the UK. As you can imagine, it was an interesting tale and certainly helped to pass the time. Kris spent time in jail for his crimes, hence the book's name, *A Little Bird*, which is a slang phrase for doing jailtime. He only had one copy of his book, which he signed and gave to Will. We chatted for the whole journey until we got off back in Goa.

When we arrived, I called my parents and told them what had happened. I mentioned my bank card and about sending it over. My dad said he would send it over ASAP. He must have mentioned the situation to my uncle, who worked in the same office as I did. My uncle told my dad a colleague of ours (Davy McCrae) was going to Goa in a couple of days and it would be quicker for him to take the card over. What a happy synchronicity.

It was about an hour's drive from where I was staying where I met Davy at his five-star all-inclusive hotel. Davy and his wife asked me to stay on for a few hours. I lapped up the luxury, free booze and food for the day. I remember Davy couldn't believe I'd arrived with no shoes on. The thing is, I'd been living on a beach for weeks and had no need for shoes. We sat and had a couple of drinks and I found out I had worked beside Davy's wife's brother at the post office. She was in recovery from cancer but sadly passed away not long after. Davy also passed away in 2022 and there was a huge turnout at his funeral for this larger-than-life man.

I thanked them both and returned to Palolem to spend the last days of my trip. I returned home a few days before Christmas. On Boxing Day, the waves hit, killing an estimated 250,000 people in many countries. My first thoughts when I heard about the tsunami were of the people who were still there, the travellers and the locals I'd met, who didn't have much to start with. I know at least some of them must have lost their lives. I also thought of those who'd robbed us for a pittance; although I didn't hold much sympathy for them at the time, thousands of people died in Unawatuna and Galle, so their chance of survival must have been slim. In hindsight, I do feel compassion for them because what must your life be like if you feel the need to rob and inflict pain on people just to survive. I wanted to return to Sri Lanka to see what I could do to help, but my family convinced me otherwise. I knew they had my best interests at heart, but I felt a sense of guilt at the time.

After the tsunami hit, it deeply affected me. Perhaps I should expand on that: after I nearly drowned, then was tied up at gunpoint, meaning I changed my plans and avoided the biggest natural disaster of our times, which most likely saved my life, it had a deep effect on me; no shit, Sherlock.

I avoided any news of the disaster for years; I just couldn't stomach it. I had a fear I would see a body of someone I'd met. Irrational, maybe, but fears can be. What I do know is that with the number of backpackers and locals I met in India and Sri Lanka, not all of them could have survived. Most of the travellers had round-the-world tickets going to destinations like Thailand, Indonesia and Sri Lanka, which were all places badly hit by the tsunami of 2004.

Once I returned home, I can only describe my behaviour as some sort of manic awakening state high, followed by a crash; some form of PTSD. In hindsight, it was a reaction to the fragility of life that I had been exposed to in these experiences. I felt quite alone, and the black dog of depression was back. I was at an all-time low after years of depression, stress and social anxiety, and with the goings-on in India, I'd had about all I could take. I started not to give a fuck about anyone or anything. I hurt a lot of people who were close to me AGAIN. I can't do anything about that now. I truly regret the decisions I made but I don't expect forgiveness from them. I can't really go into details, as I don't want to cause any further hurt or embarrassment. Let's just say, I was a complete arsehole to people really close to me.

After a few months, the ultimate lesson I was to learn from the near misses and striking synchronicities in India sank in. It was the universe shouting, "STEVE, YOU FUCKING DOUGHNUT, TIME TO MAKE SOME CHANGES!"

Prior to the India/Sri Lanka trip, I had been drifting through life like a boat without a rudder for years. I needed to drop the anchor and just find some space before trying to bring some peacefulness and a bit more direction to my life. A bit like I'd done when I went to Newcastle eight years earlier.

I had to face facts: numbing the pain with substances hadn't worked, the passage of time hadn't worked, I needed professional help, I needed this shit out of my head. In 2005, after being off sick with depression, I sought help through an employee assistance programme that offered free counselling. This would be pivotal in my recovery, but it was a slow process and only the beginning of healing my brokenness.

Prior to starting the counselling sessions, I had met with my uncle Cliff as he was concerned for my welfare. I remember saying, "I don't know if I can carry on anymore." I wouldn't call it suicidal ideation, but I was ready to give up on life, so maybe it was. I knew I wouldn't carry it through, as I had a son and family who, no matter how much pain I was feeling, I wouldn't give up on. A few years later, a good friend and flatmate of mine took his own life and it made me wonder how many people's troubles go unnoticed or unhelped? It leaves behind a trail of despair for those left behind when people follow through on taking their own life. It's a sad state of societal affairs when this is the option a human takes to stop the pain.

I knew that I needed to try something, and counselling was what I went with. I went along not knowing where to start; I'm sure a lot of people are like that. Every week, I'd get the bus along to the sessions and I'd think, *I really have nothing more to say*, and every week I would come out crying. These sessions slowly let me get to grip with everything from my self-worth to why I had acted the way I did in the past and present. Please don't misunderstand, this wasn't a get-out clause for my behaviour, but it let me understand it better and I slowly let the self-judgement go.

Three words finally broke the dam of emotion. I remember the counsellor asking me, "So how did you feel when your partner left you, you felt you couldn't be a responsible father and you got your family into debt?" SHAME AND HUMILIATION was my response and I started bawling my eyes out and couldn't stop; it was like a floodgate of tears had been waiting for fourteen years to come out. This was just the start of it. I started to talk about how ever since I could remember I'd always felt stupid and not good enough. This release gave me a springboard to push on further down the recovery highway.

It wasn't until recently that I realised that all I had ever done was attach a story to an event. All I needed to do to change this was to tell a different story.

Example event: I wasn't very academic.

The story I told myself was I was a failure, stupid and not enough because my grades were so bad. I had evidence as people told me that and I told myself that.

Solution, tell a different story: I did understand subjects, I just found it hard to put it down on paper > I wasn't dumb, I just needed to learn in a unique way and not believe my own self-limiting beliefs > take my time and focus.

If you think about it, all the views that we hold of ourselves are just opinions. These opinions have been conditioned and reinforced in our minds throughout our lives as we walk around looking for events that prove us correct. It's complete madness, really, our minds would rather be correct about our perceived inadequacies causing us pain than realise the truth, that it's all just a story in our heads. If you don't like the story you're living, live a different one and, with practice, you can.

In hindsight, I'm glad for the mental struggles I had and may have in the future. It's only through these struggles that I forged and will forge meaning in my life.

You may think hindsight is a wonderful thing, it's easy to look back and say it was worthwhile, but this view has no validity when you are living through the crises. I conceded that there is truth in this view, but once you've lived through those dark times and come out on the other side, it makes dealing with any future hardships easier to accept. If you believe that the traumas you live through are only life presenting an opportunity for you to learn and grow, it makes it a lot easier to process and even live through the situation.

If you accept that in the future you'll look back and say, "Ah, that's why that happened, and here's what I learned," wouldn't this be better than the victim narrative of "why is this happening to me" or "why did this happen to me"?

I'm not saying that on day one of dealing with the pain you can simply flick a switch and all will be rosy in your life, but once you are ready to deal with mental pain, it can be a major source of strength for you and other people in your life.

I know I'm likely to get a lot of "what-aboutery" comments on this view, saying you can't say that in this or that situation, and that's fine, let's agree to have a different opinion. I can only say what I've learned relative to working through my own issues. Please don't get upset about it, as you're the one who must deal with the anger, not me, and that's not what either of us want.

Some people might say, "Steve, what are you talking about when you say, 'life is presenting you with situations for you to learn and grow from'?" And you may think it's a crock of shit. I'll ask you this question: have you ever known someone who makes the same mistake repeatedly in life? Or the same circumstances continue to happen to them? And you think "just move on or get to the point, [insert situation] is bad for you", but they don't seem to get it?

Well, that's what I'm talking about. They are not learning the lesson, so life keeps throwing it back in their face until they do. In fact, some people never learn. This isn't a criticism. In fact, I've been that person many times. But, now I'm aware of it, I can work through it, instead of crying *why me*! Awareness is the first step, followed by analysis of what you need to learn, followed by application. It sounds easy but it's fucking hard! And that's the point, nothing that's worthwhile tends to be easy.

But isn't it better to have a view and try to change it for the better? Opposed to living in *Groundhog Day*, blaming everyone or the circumstances around you over and over again? Or saying that's just the way things are, only to perpetually stay in the same scene in the play of life and never progress.

I was now ready to plant some roots and put some effort into my work life, I wanted more from what life had to offer.

CHAPTER 13

Laying Foundations for Stability

After two years of working through the shit in my head, in 2007, I bought a flat. This was with the help from my cousin Scott, who has always been like a brother to me. I now had a home again; I had been living in flat shares since selling my flat and really needed my own space. I needed time and space to build solid foundations for my life. As the saying goes, if you build your house on quicksand, it's going to sink. I'd been living with shoddy foundations for too long.

I needed a place where I could fend for myself and really prove to myself I was capable of coping with life, without the fear of impending doom. Looking back, it was about learning to make better choices; the better choices I made, the better outcomes arrived at my door. Simple, really, but something that had passed me by in my younger years.

It was tough going financially, even with renting a room out to my mate Grant. I didn't have that much disposable income to start with, but I had enough to get by and had some great times in that flat.

It was time to put some effort into my career and, in 2009, 2012, 2016 and 2019, I gained promotions at work. I had never really placed much effort into my career before this time because when you suffer from depression you see no point. *What's the point, I'll still feel shit; what's the point, I'll fail anyway, I always do.* The counselling shone some light through the cracks and changed my view. These promotions came with a financial reward, of course, which meant I could start having nicer things.

There's one decision that stands out for me that really made a difference. I had gained two promotions by this point and had been asked if I wanted to take up a management role. This was a sideways move for no extra money, and at the time, I thought, *Do I really want to take on extra responsibility for no financial reward?* It was a standout decision for me, as it was the first time in my life that I decided to take the harder route in life with no visible reward. My instincts were telling me to do it and that was good enough for me.

I'd always been a path of least resistance person, a "couldn't be bothered with the hassle" sort of guy, or more like an "if I don't try, I won't fail" sort of person. Failure was a painful thing to me in my past, instead of the learning process it is now. I learned not to make it personal if things don't work out.

I went from managing people to managing people who manage people, to managing people who manage people who manage people. Or, in simpler terms, I gained another couple of promotions. I really enjoy the role; it can be challenging at times but has its rewards, and I'm not just talking about financial ones. Part of the job is helping people when they are struggling both professionally and personally, and I believe this is where my thoughts of doing this as a career stemmed from.

CHAPTER 14

Partner in Crime

I had dated on and off through my adult life but there was nothing that could be called a meaningful relationship. It could never turn into anything serious, how could it? Prior to 2006, I didn't have a great view of myself or of life. The on-off part continued as I tried online dating for a while, which consisted of loads of dates, loads of fun, but for whatever reason, the right person just wasn't to be found. It gave me more confidence, though, and ultimately, I believe it happened that way because it just wasn't the right time.

In 2011, I finally met my wife Anneke. We met online but it wasn't a dating platform, it was a music group on Facebook. When we met, we were both still on the boozy train. Anneke had had a rough couple of years and was going out a few nights a week like I was. This eventually calmed down and, by 2017, which is the year we got married, quiet nights in were the order of the day. Although, when we did get out, it was never for a quiet drink, it was always full steam ahead.

We moved from the flat I owned with Scott into a house with a garden and some private space. Oh yeah, I should have said, we got a cat in 2016 – can't forget Audrey!

You'd think that would be enough. Life, though, had other ideas!

In the material and emotional worlds, I had built a comfortable life, although I still had that nagging that there was something more I should be doing. I now know "should" isn't the best word, as it comes from a place of obligation and lack. I wouldn't work that out until much later, though, so "should" was where I was back then.

It was in 2019 that life gave me another gentle nudge to say, "Okay, you've done well, but the outer world is not all that exists." In typical synchronisation fashion, it would be in India again that this would be revealed.

CHAPTER 15

India, the Return

In 2017, I got married to my lovely wife Anneke. We held our wedding in the Scottish borders and it was a genuinely great celebration. The location and venue were brilliant and, to add a personal touch, Anneke's sister Katie was the celebrant who married us. Katie is an amazing orator and the way she delivered our and her words was something special.

Getting married not only gained me a wife but new sisters, brothers, a mum- and dad-in-law. The Deverell family made me most welcome. I even became an uncle; having no siblings, this was a new experience for me.

We had just bought a house before we got married and were due to move in a month after the wedding – talk about taking on a lot of stressful situations at once. It all turned out well in the end, but what with the expense of a new home, we couldn't really afford the honeymoon we wanted. We decided that when we could afford a honeymoon, we would travel to India; Anneke had a desire to go there, and I always knew I would return one day.

We saved until 2019 when we took a month-long trip to India, starting off in Delhi and going on to Agra, Jaipur, Kerala in October and ending up back in Goa in November. It was a complete contrast to the booze-filled adventure in 2004; it was truly an immense trip that we both enjoyed. Things mostly went to plan but the rainy season hadn't really left Goa, which was unusual for November. The day before we were due to arrive in Patnam, a cyclone hit. When we got there, the place we were due to stay at called Turtle Hill was in bits. The manager found us a great replacement called Abi Dahl, which had a very chilled out owner called Ben.

On our first day, I checked the weather. There were two cyclones out in the Arabian sea heading towards us again. This was the first time that two cyclones had developed at the same time in the Arabian sea in recorded history – what is it with me, this part of the world and natural phenomena? Luckily, they moved off and went in the other direction, leaving us to ten days of sunny weather.

I did say things *mostly* went to plan. We did have one incident that we haven't really told many people about. Again, it involved another natural phenomenon – the sea. We were staying on Agonda Beach on the 4th of November, which was our last day in Goa before flying back to Delhi for a night and onwards back to the UK. We went for a swim in pleasant-looking stretch of water. We had been in for a while when I noticed Anneke was a bit away from me. I could tell things weren't right, she was in trouble, and you guessed it, it was with my old nemesis the rip current. I had thoughts of losing Anneke on our honeymoon and swam as fast as I could towards her. I tried to calm her down, told her to relax and said when the waves arrive, swim like mad parallel to the shore. I kept hold of her and we both went onto our backs and kicked like mad.

After a short while, I could feel the bottom with my feet. I grabbed Anneke and dragged her towards the shore. It was over quicker than my time in Sri Lanka, but it didn't make it any less frightening for Anneke and for me thinking of what might have happened. The key is: it didn't happen. We made our way back to the hotel and we didn't really discuss it, we just carried on. It was totally weird but that's what we did.

On the 7th of November, we arrived home. The next day, whilst checking the local news, I saw a headline that caught my eye about a local man who had died in a shark attack whilst on holiday in the Indian Ocean. I clicked on the story and, to my horror, found that it was someone I knew and had worked with closely for ten years. Later reports said Richard may have drowned after getting into difficulties. They only recovered his arm in the belly of a tiger shark, so it was thought that the shark had eaten him post-mortem after his body was washed out to sea. Well, I choose to believe that's what happened.

My heart goes out to Richard's wife, family and friends; he truly was a unique man and when I think of him it always raises a smile to my face.

Two days later, another man was found drowned in a shallow lagoon, with no evidence of an attack, adding to the credence that both were accidental drownings by some unknown currents. Reading the story, the incident had happened around the same time as ours. I'm in the same region again, something life-threatening happens to me in the water and someone I know loses their life again. I hadn't really thought about the tsunami in a long time, but I started to think about some of the locals and travellers I'd met who must have perished. I also thought about what could have been on that beach in Agonda had I not noticed Anneke in trouble.

In January of 2020, I formed the opinion that life was giving me a kick up the ass yet again. On the face of it, my life looked good: a well-paid job, amazing wife, nice house, great friends. There was still a feeling of something missing and "not enough"-ness.

In my younger years, my "I've let people down before" opinion had manifested in a negative way. For instance, I wouldn't want to push myself at work in case I failed, and I let folk down. This would be using that energy in a negative way, but it can also be used for positive outcomes. What I did was take my thoughts of "I've let people down" (past tense) and flipped it to "I'm not allowed to let people down" (future tense). I had taken the same energy and used it as a driving force to gain four promotions at work. The problem was that it doesn't deal with the fear inside and it needs constant success to keep it at bay.

The years from 2020 to 2023 would be when I would finally dissolve the negative thoughts of letting folk down and "not enough"-ness inside of me. In part two, we'll find out how I did that.

Part 2

Sort Out the Mind
and the Rest Will Follow

CHAPTER 16

Healing the Brokenness

2020-2023

I n certain spiritual circles, people believe that all of us are born broken to some degree. The game of life is about healing that brokenness through learning the lessons life throws at us. If we don't learn, we continually react the same way, display the same behaviours, get the same results, and when these results do not align with what we want, we suffer. The more conventional thought is our brokenness is learned.

I think it's a bit of both. The mountain is there to be climbed, our challenges are there to be accepted and overcome; get your boots on, it's time to hike.

I want to share the things I did to heal my brokenness. Before I get to that, I'd like to define brokenness. For me, it was the "not enough"-ness in life and other feelings of inadequacy. For others, it might be being socially awkward or lacking in confidence. The hints and tips in the following pages could be applied to you, no matter what your brokenness is.

It's also important to say that healing does not mean getting rid of unpleasant emotions or feelings. It's about accepting how we feel when we feel it and realising we all feel the so-called "negative" or "darker" emotions and feelings in life. It's from this point we can be with our challenges and move through them, rather than trying to destroy them.

I suppose I've been healing me for a long time, meandering through life, picking up learnings to plug the hole, peeling away layers of the clichéd onion, which is a never-ending task at times. However, in the years 2020-2023, I made more progress than in the previous twenty. I want to help others, and this is the main driver of this book, not just to tell my story.

If you've ever thought that you were:
- a failure
- not enough
- unlovable
- stupid
- negative minded.

Or, if you've thought *my life is shit, it will always be shit and that's that*. Well, the next few chapters might help to change this view or at least inspire you to change. I don't have a magic pill to resolve things overnight or all the answers, I can only tell you what worked for me.

Lazy ass warning: it does require some effort but I'm living proof that you can change, as at one point or another I have thought of myself as all these things.

It may also include concepts that some people find hard to accept and that's fine. I can only call it as I see it or, more accurately, as I feel it, but I hope you find them of some use.

In the next chapter, it's time to get down with discussing what we all want: to be happy. Even if we think we want something else, it's happiness we all seek.

CHAPTER 17

I'll Have Five Kilos of
Your Finest Happiness Please

Most people in life want to be happy. I had lived most of my life falling into the trap of saying, "When X happens then I'll be happy," but funnily enough, no matter what I achieved or what positive things happened to me, there was still a feeling of *there's something missing*.

Here's just some things I told myself. When I:

- get that job
- buy those trainers
- gain a promotion
- gain another promotion
- own my own house
- own a bigger house
- earn X amount of money
- travel

THEN I WILL BE HAPPY!

The thing is these achievements will only ever give you an approximation of happiness. It may make you happy for a while, but over time, that will fade, and you are back to square one, chasing the happiness horse down the racetrack of life. The problem is the horse is faster than you and is always out of reach. I've done all the things I listed, none of them erased that feeling that there's something missing, at best I got a temporary buzz.

I was subconsciously telling myself I needed to pursue happiness and find it in a defined set of circumstances. Let's look at the statement: the pursuit of happiness. The fact that you are seeking something must mean you don't have it now or, in other words, you are in lack. In turn, this means you are saying that happiness must be in the future, and you are not complete as you are. But we don't live in the future, so it causes mental discomfort in the here and now. When I got or achieved X, I would get a small relief. I would then transfer my thinking to the next thing, falsely believing *then I'll be happy*.

It goes a little something like this:

Attach happiness to a goal > achieve the goal in the future > sense of happiness via achievement > happiness subsides > lack of happiness > causes suffering through want > back to the beginning.

It doesn't mean you don't have goals, and yes, fully commit to your goals, but don't invest your happiness in the outcome of them. At best, the happiness will be short-lived (and that's if you succeed). This logic even applies to a person, but we'll get to that in a bit. I now believe the pursuit of happiness in the external world is a load of bollocks; it can only be found in oneself, and in the present, as that is where we live.

It means don't run down the racetrack chasing the happiness horse. Stay still, go nowhere and look inside. That may sound a bit woo and triggering for some people but that's where I found happiness – inside, as part of me – and in essence happiness is who we all are.

The statement "know thyself" has been around for a very long time for a reason, as it is a road to many things we seek, like wisdom, truth, inner peace and happiness. "I DON'T KNOW WHO I AM!" I hear you scream. Don't worry, neither do most people. Taking up practices such as meditation, yoga, EFT and breathwork were just some of the ways I found a path back to me and happiness. There are other things I did as well, like finding a sense of community and I stopped drinking alcohol. Don't worry, I'm not expecting you to do all these things; you need to find what works for you.

So, let's look at a few happiness scenarios.

Imagine I'm a genie and could grant you one wish and you ask for unlimited money to spend.

Imagine I now said I could grant you that wish but I need to let you know it would make you terribly unhappy in life, would you still want that wish? Everyone I've asked that question has said no, they wouldn't take the money if it meant they'd be miserable.

What this demonstrates is that it's not the money that's wanted, it's the happiness you believe the money will bring. Therefore, it's happiness you really want, not money.

This is the same for any wish you asked for; a partner, job, house. Would you still want it if you knew it would make you unhappy? I think not.

I suppose you could ask the wish to be that you were happy all your life, but how would you know you were happy without knowing unhappiness? And how much would have to be prevented to keep you happy? For example, when we meet a partner who we love and live with all our life, they or we will one day be gone, as we are all heading in the same direction (death). So, investing your happiness in people doesn't work.

Some people might say what a morbid way to look at things. I don't think it is. You could look at that fact, acknowledge it as a truth, and live your life together to the fullest. Two ways of looking at the same event, one negative, one positive. Either way, the outcome is inevitable, ignoring it won't help.

Placing your happiness in others or things is setting yourself up for failure, as the only constant is change and that's where we can feel loss. This is what Buddhists mean when they say attachment causes suffering. This doesn't mean don't have things or relationships, just don't invest your happiness in them and become attached to them.

If you look closer at the love you feel for someone, you might find it emanates from a different source. People mistakenly ascribe the love they feel for their partner as something that their partner gives to them, believing once they are gone, then the love will be gone. I had everything, a beautiful wife, great job, enough money, lovely house, great family, but I still felt as though things weren't right. Why? Because I didn't know who I was, and what I did know I only partially understood. After a lot of "project me" work, I realised something: the love I feel comes from within me and is me, my wife is a mirror who reflects and reveals this love back to me.

It's about recognising that, growing it and you being the example love of the world and your own source of happiness. I'm not talking about the definition of love we see in the movies. This is about seeing the other as you, creating a connection to yourself and realising the oneness of the world and all things.

I'm one for basing my beliefs in experiences; I've experienced this, so I believe it to be true. You may not have experienced it and don't accept it to be true. If we're honest, we both don't know 100%, but at least be open to the suggestion that it might be true; wouldn't you like it to be? Well, you can once you believe it to be.

These realisations didn't come to me overnight, and I don't claim them all as mine, they happened after three years of meditation, yoga practice and picking up concepts from studying many teachers. At first, it was something I came to understand as a concept, then latterly began to feel it to be true. The experiential part had the most impact, of course – when you have personal evidence it's easier to buy into something.

If you'd told me I'd be writing this in a book a few years ago, talking about knowing oneself, I'd have laughed at you. But there we have it, people change, opinions change, but only if we are willing to seek our truth.

I have more work to do on myself and my shadow side to embrace, but I'm enjoying climbing the mountain now, instead of resisting what life throws at me. I see the challenges as my teachers. We are here to learn how to be, let's enjoy it.

I now know that I am the happiness I was looking for, what did I do to get there? Let's find out.

CHAPTER 18

Reframing My Perspective

The first step I took on my journey was sorting the perspective I'd held about myself.

A big step in doing this is to accept how things are right now, however bad your current circumstance. Things might not be great or might even be desperate, but acceptance of your current reality is a starting block for change. This might sound a very cold view when we are talking about someone passing or coming out of an abusive relationship. I'm not saying that during these events you should just pick yourself up, focus on this and boom, you'll be fine, that would be ridiculous. Once you have created the space to deal with the emotional attachment to the circumstance, you can then accept the situation and face it as "shit that happened" and start to think about moving on.

If you do hold on to the memory of a bad situation without dealing with it, it will cause resistance, which in turn will cause internal turmoil. Most of us know this to some degree when we say, "You need to let it go." (I'm sure there's a song about that.) But practising what we know is a different matter.

Acceptance of the situation through facing it was key for me. It's not the circumstance itself that causes the mental turmoil, it's the emotional attachment or story I gave to the situation. This view also doesn't mean that you become apathetic to life, accept everything and let people walk over you. If someone was hurting your child, for instance, you'd need to act for sure. I'm talking all the things we make a big issue when they aren't physically or life-threatening, but we mentally torture ourselves as though they are. We need to look at disentangling the stories we tell ourselves versus what is happening and has happened.

Let's look at this example on circumstance and perspective: two people buy identical watches that cost £5,000, and they both lose their watches the next day. The first person is really pissed off as he saved for years to buy that watch. The second person doesn't really care as he is a millionaire and has many watches, so he can just easily buy another one. The circumstance is the same – both lost identical watches – it's the perspective and emotional attachment that differ. In the case of the first person, it's the resistance to what happened that causes the suffering and changes the situation compared to the millionaire.

Put another way, it's the story (their thoughts) about the situation that were different. In turn, their reactions were different, therefore their outcomes were different – one person raging, the other doesn't care.

The blame game is also a pitfall you want to avoid:

pointing to someone or a circumstance and saying they are or that is to blame for how you feel is just nuts. You are in control of your reactions and feelings. It might not excuse what they did, but letting anger turn into blame and then resentment is only affecting one person, you. Being correct doesn't dismiss the resentment you'll feel afterwards.

As for judging, this is you expecting people to live up to your standards and, when they don't, you get upset. How mad is that? You are saying they need to know what you think, and live or act the way you want them to, or you'll have a problem. Who put you in charge?

Most people will have heard that you are not your thoughts; the problem is that hardly anybody lives that way. We live as though we are our thoughts. *I'm a failure, I'm not enough, I'm unlovable*. These are the common thoughts or stories we tell ourselves; we even provide evidence to prove to ourselves and others how inadequate we are. The good news is if you don't like the story you are telling, then you can tell a different one, you're the author.

I had tortured myself with these thoughts throughout my life, but now I've learned to catch myself, and you know what I'm going to say, right? Yip, it takes practice.

In the past, I'd look at a personal circumstance, point to it and internally shout *failure, failure, failure* to myself. An example of something I reframed was the relationship break-up with my son's mother. The original version of what I told myself was *she walked out on us, I'm a failure to her and my son*. I also thought to myself, *I must be to blame for this, otherwise she wouldn't have left*. All that happened was she just wasn't around anymore. It's the attached story and emotion to the event that caused suffering, not the event itself, and guess who's in control of my reaction or the story attached to the emotional side of things? Yes, me!

I held a lot of resentment towards her leaving my son and me, but resentment is like drinking poison and expecting the other person to suffer. This story is years in the past for me. Why? Because I forgave the situation, reframed it as she wasn't around anymore, it wasn't to be and moved on. We both only acted to the best of our ability, but it wasn't enough to make it work, why? Because that's the only thing we could do and that's the outcome that happened. There is no person to blame, regardless of the actions of ourselves or others!

The odd thing is, until recently, I had never analysed what I did during my counselling years ago that reprogrammed my mind about that scenario. If I had, I could have applied that logic to all the other "I'm not good enough/failure" scenarios I had in my head, but I didn't. No use worrying about it now.

We tell ourselves, *If only it had been this way*, or, *It should have worked out that way*. The should've, could've, would've need to get chucked into the bin! They are no good. Why? There's only ever what did happen or is happening, and we need to accept it, or we'll feel the pain of resistance.

It was my reality at the time that the break-up was a hurtful thing, and I applied a bad label to it. If it hadn't happened, then I wouldn't be living the life I am now, which is my happy life with Anneke, so it wasn't all bad, it turned out good.

It also harks back to my Sri Lankan experiences. Something I thought to be "bad" happened (the robbery) but this saved my life (missing the tsunami), so you could view it as a "good thing". In fact, to take it a step further, none of this is bad or good, it just IS.

The acceptance of the truth (what happened or reality), not the subjective (my story of what happened) was the key to shifting my perspective on all the evidence I had for the "I'm not enough, I'm a failure and unlovable" head chatter I had.

I hope this shows what imposters bad and good labels are and how the thoughts we have are at best an opinion. This IS what's happening and that IS what happened, there is no good or bad unless I make that association. I accept that in everyday language using terms good or bad are useful, but it doesn't always make them accurate or a truth.

At the time, my relationship break-up affected me deeply. The fallout from this meant I developed a fear of loss and overcompensated by becoming an over-attentive people pleaser. I would smother new partners with love or friends with attention, which is counterproductive, as these actions come from a place of fear of losing them, not love. In turn, people would sense this and the relationships would end, or I'd not seem genuine. This, in turn, supplied more evidence of failure for my ego to bang on about in my head, telling me how correct it was.

What a fucking dick the ego and thoughts generated by

it can be! But not anymore, as I won't let it be. No more will I be ruled by my thoughts, it's the heart that knows best and this is where I now make my decisions.

Guilt is another thing we can suffer from; it's like an illness that we cause ourselves. I'm sure if you have ever been a parent, then you will have experienced guilt at some point. A frequent occurrence of guilt would be when we have to say no to our child, but they don't understand why and get upset. It's doesn't have to be as a parent you feel guilt, it can be because you should or shouldn't have done something. (Remember, we've discussed should and shouldn't have before – get it in the bin!)

In my case, my biggest source of guilt was as a father. When my son was young, I couldn't be the dad I wanted to be, I wasn't mature enough. I looked at my behaviours and attitude back then and thought, *What sort of role model was I?* I was someone with a chip on their shoulder, who thought that success should come without effort. I was angry at the world; I would drink too much and didn't have the financial or emotional faculty to allow my son to stay with me.

My son was raised by my parents, although I will give myself some due, I was in the same house where we shared a room until my son was eight. I moved out then as it was apparent we both needed our own space. When he grew up, he had issues of his own, which of course I blamed myself for and felt more guilt about being such a shit role model.

So, that was the bag of guilt that I dragged around.

Why do we do this to ourselves? All of that had already happened, none of it could be changed, but years later the voice in my head was saying, *You were a shit dad*. Even if it were true, how is that going to help the situation now?

Think about something you did years ago that you still feel guilty about? Why do you torture yourself? And remember, this is just your version of what happened and may not be how others see it.

I came to realise a few things about this guilt during my healing process:

1. When my son became an adult, I spoke to him about it and he thought he had a great childhood.
2. I acted to the best of my understanding at that time.
3. What's happened has happened and couldn't have happened any other way. Why? Because it didn't. (Peter Crone, The Mind Architect).
4. Punishing myself for something years in the past was idiotic as it wouldn't help the me living now.
5. Having learned one through four, it was time to release all my guilt.

If you have guilt, it is something I would recommend working on using the logic above. Nobody ever became the best version of themselves dragging a bag of guilt with them. How long do you have to suffer for a mistake? Six months, six years?

This doesn't mean go around acting like a dick as there's no point in guilt – so sorry, I'm not giving you a get out of jail free card. To modernise a Saint Augustine quote, you need to "love and do whatever you want", so going around causing harm is out of the question.

And finally, we get to comparing yourself to others. Yes, been there done that too!

- I'm not as good as the best person, so I shouldn't do it.
- They have more than me, that's not fair.
- What do I have to offer compared to them?

These are just some of the ways we like to kick ourselves in the balls (or baby maker if you're a woman). A common one is putting ourselves down as someone is better than us, so why bother? Well do bother, you have a uniqueness of your own that may resonate with someone.

Imagine you wanted to do a particular self-employed job, but the market was saturated with people working in that field, so you think, *I shouldn't bother, there's too many people doing it, they've been doing it longer, they will be better than me, ahh I'll just stick with what I've got.* This is just the ego monkey up to its mind fuckery again (get it in the bin). If you are ever going to compare yourself, then compare yourself to you yesterday, not someone else today. Have you improved? Yes, pat yourself on the back and ask how you can improve more today. If the answer is no, then what do you need to do to improve today? Thinking about it only takes you so far, and action is needed after thought.

What other people are doing is nothing to do with you. The only thing you should be focusing on is what is within your control (you) not what is not (other people).

There are lots and lots of ways to take small steps to

reprogramme your mind to a different outlook. You've learned to think the way you do, and you can unlearn it. How do I know? Because I did reprogram the way I think.

Please don't get me wrong, I still deal with anger and negative self-talk; guilt and judgement thoughts still pop into my head from time to time – I am human, after all. But I now have an early warning system built in through practice, which catches these thoughts and emotions. Instead of dwelling on things for hours, weeks or even years and letting it spiral downward, I deal with them as they arise.

How did I do this? I read books on personal development that resonated with me. Now given that I'd hardly read a book since *The Very Hungry Caterpillar* when I was five, if I can do it, you can. Due to my slow reading skills, I found podcasts and audiobooks worked even better. Two of the main teachers whose mind concepts resonated with me were Peter Crone and Eckhart Tolle.

Peter is known as The Mind Architect; I listened to every podcast I could with him on it and completed his Free Your Mind and Free Your Future courses. I applied Peter's work to my life and that's where I picked up reframing the situations that I'd been telling myself. Peter's words were like an epiphany; in fact, it was an orgasm of epiphanies.

Peter has a direct approach, a bit like me, which is why his reframing of our thoughts and language struck a chord of clarity in my mind. He made me realise that the limitations I think I have are only there through my programmed prospective of life. One of his quotes that stuck in my mind (and there are many) was: "Failure is at best an event, not a person."

Eckhart Tolle helped bring the concept of living in the now to my life. My mind would swing back and forth from regrets in the past to fears in the future. But, as I've said before, none of us live in the past or future, it's all stories in our head associated with fear and regret, or at best daydreams. Living like this means we get stuck and miss the only thing we ever live in, the now.

As a starting point to changing your outlook, I'd look at both Peter and Eckhart's work. There's plenty of their content on YouTube, they both have websites[2] and books. From the centre of my heart, I'd like to thank them both. Without them, I would have been going round in circles for the rest of my life.

After I had already reprogrammed my mind, I found Gerry Murphy and Lorraine Buchanan's book *Now I Understand: A Guide to Life in Layman's Terms*. Gerry is a Scotsman from Glasgow whose story went from suffering from mental illness, drink and drug abuse to being an inspirational speaker, author and helping people to heal themselves. Our stories were different but our realisations of how much shit we tell ourselves and conclusions on how to change it were similar. The book goes into these concepts in more depth than I have in this chapter.

Sorting the mind is the start, as there's no use starting healthy pursuits if the mind monkeys are constantly

---

2   www.petercrone.com, www.eckharttolle.com

limiting you with their chatter. But now I've pointed you in the right direction, we should look at the pursuits that worked for me.

All aboard the part-route bus to enlightenment!

Part 3

Finding New Interests

CHAPTER 19

Meditation

I t's odd, many times in my life I've thought, *That's me now, I've figured it out, I've dealt with my demons*, only for depression to turn up again, or I feel a sense of lack or just that sense that something is missing.

As I sit here typing this in 2023, these are things of the past. Why am I so confident that things are different this time? Well, over and above knowing who I am and not listening to the mind monkeys anymore, I am living in alignment with who I am. When you do that, magically, things start to gravitate towards you, the universe listens and your life changes for the better.

Who am I? Well, I'm not the self-deprecating thoughts. They are like waves at the top of the ocean, and through meditation I found stillness beneath them. In the stillness, I found myself. When I hear my mind saying: *You can't, it will fail, you will fail, people won't like you, you'll get in trouble*, etc., where do I put them? That's correct: in the bin!

That doesn't mean these feelings, emotions and limitations don't come up, I just face them for what they are, opinions of the ego. The limiting opinions of others, too: get it in the bin!

I'm not saying I'm sitting on my yoga mat levitating every day (well, not much), but in the last few years I have found some great tools that have improved my inner sense of peace. Meditation being one of them.

I still feel the urge to launch the laptop across the room when it doesn't do what I want it to for the tenth time in a row. But now I calm my mind a lot quicker by going inside and taming the wild horse that lives there. I'm in charge, not my thoughts. I think from my heart a lot more, instead of my head. Instead of using my masculine energy to fix my way through the problem, I use the feminine, asking how it would make me feel if I did X or Y, and if the answer is negative, I don't do it.

Being more instead of *doing* has helped me navigate life better! There is nothing wrong with doing, but you need a balance, something I didn't have before.

If you are currently fifty percent content in life, wouldn't it be good to become ninety-six percent? Improvement doesn't mean perfection, and to quote The Mind Architect Peter Crone, "Don't become perfect, you won't have anybody to relate to."

If you are sitting reading this book thinking, *I want to change, I'm sick of X in my life*, then you can do it, but you can't do it by being the same person, continuing the same habits, thinking the same negative thoughts, being around the same toxic people. To become the new you, you need to change your behaviours, outlook and even sometimes the people in your life. You can't expect things to change if you don't.

After reprogramming my conscious mind to accept my past and not worrying about the future, it was time to find positive activities. It's important to find things you have an interest in. If you find something you love, it's never a chore. How do you find something you love? By trying as many things as you think you'd like. If you don't like it, ditch it, if you do like it, stick with it.

At the end of January 2020, I took up meditation, as I had always wanted to try it. It was just as well I did as the coming months were going to be very testing indeed. This was the start of the transformation of me.

I started my meditation journey using the Calm app, which had a seven- and twenty-eight-day programme for beginners. The app introduced me to several types of meditation techniques. It also cleared up a lot of the common misconceptions surrounding meditation, such as:

- Only certain people can meditate.
- Having a busy mind means I can't meditate.
- Meditation is about having no thoughts.
- You must be religious or sit in a cave all day to do it.
- A Scotsman who likes football can't do it.

After about three months, I started seeing some benefits and I loved doing it. I could get to sleep easier, and I didn't need as much sleep. I started meditating for five minutes a day, then by three months I was up to twenty minutes twice a day.

Six months in, I also had an unexpected effect of meditation – memories of the past came back to me. These memories were where I felt I was dumb or had let folk down with feelings of loneliness, which made me feel uneasy. When you look inward, it's not all roses and butterflies – sometimes it's thorns and snakes. This wasn't pleasant at the time, but I'd already worked on the conscious part of the programme and meditation gave insight to my subconscious part. Given that our minds run 90% of the time subconsciously, understanding and dealing with these final bits of negative chatter could only benefit me.

As I'm sure you are aware, 2020 was the year Covid struck and, two months after I took up meditation, in March 2020, the UK went into full lockdown. This added pressures in my life, which were:

- Not being able to see family and friends.
- Being locked in my house for twenty-three hours per day with one hour of exercise.
- During this period my dad was waiting for a heart operation, so in the high-risk category for Covid.
- Everything at work was going into meltdown, we couldn't manage the amount of work we had and, as the manager, I felt a personal responsibility for that.
- People within the team I managed were also struggling with lockdown pressures, including severe illnesses, family death and their own mental struggles. It was heartbreaking to hear.
- The brokenness I still felt.

It was these combined factors that pushed me to beyond my breaking point with stress and anxiety. At the end of 2020, I had to go off sick from work for ten weeks. I don't blame anybody; I now know that I created my own stress with my resistance and reaction to circumstances.

It was also time to start healing the brokenness inside.

From this, I took that I needed to go through it so I could learn how to deal with my reactions and views on circumstance. Taking ownership of your own shit is the hard choice but it's the correct one; it's too easy to point the finger.

You might think, *How can I promote meditation if I got stressed whilst practising it? It must not work.* All I can say is the times I meditated during this period were a huge benefit to me, giving me relief from the stress and anxiety. These two things are not mutually exclusive, you can still suffer from stress as someone who meditates. Meditation may not always be an antidote to stress (depending on the levels), but it is a medicine for it. It's not lost on me that the time I had taken up meditation coincided with the time I needed it the most.

In hindsight, I had been trying to be the best of everything in my life for years; husband, dad, employee, friend, manager. Anything short of that wasn't good enough. I mean, how unrealistic was I being to myself? I had always seen my role as a person who solved problems for those around me. It was another way I derived self-worth and, because that's what I was putting out into the universe (I'm a problem solver), then that's what the universe gave me: PROBLEMS.

The more I solved, the more problems would get

thrown my way, until my head popped, and I realised: *I CAN'T BE PERFECT AND SOLVE ALL PROBLEMS!*

I found meditation a great source of strength and I decided to take a teacher training course with the British School of Meditation in the spring of 2021. This would coincide with me returning to work refreshed and ready to go, albeit with a different outlook towards my role as chief problem solver.

As part of the course, we delved into the science behind the practice, what happens to your body when you meditate and changes in your brainwaves and activities.

I found the subject so fascinating. Fig 1 and Fig 2 are visual representations of my brainwaves. They show what happens to your brain whilst reading a book and meditating. These graphs were made by using something called a muse headband, which reads your brainwave patterns. I recorded my brainwaves and used an app called Mind Monitor developed by James Clutterbuck to produce graphs of them.

Fig 1

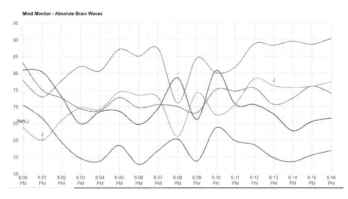

Fig 1 is a graph of my brainwaves whilst reading a book. It shows the distinct types of brainwaves the brain produces. As you can see, it's like a pile of spaghetti.

These brainwaves range from delta – the slowest frequency waves that you might experience when dreaming – up to gamma, which are the high frequency waves during times of super focus.

Due to the constraints of publishing, the graphs are in black and white, so I can't go into the details of each graph as referring to coloured lines won't make much sense to you. What you can see when comparing the two graphs is my brainwaves in Fig 2 are a lot more organised than in Fig 1.

Fig 2

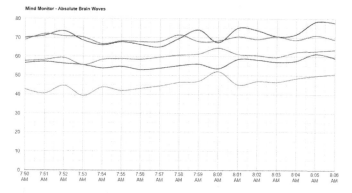

Fig 2 is a scan of my brainwaves whilst meditating. The first thing you will notice is how in phase – aka in sync – the waves have become. There is a lot more order to them. There are more alpha and delta waves, which are associated with deep rest. These are the two lines running through the top of the graph.

Alpha waves induce feelings of calm, increase creativity and enhance your ability to absorb new information. So, getting your head full of these waves a couple of times per day has so many benefits.

Here are some of them:

- Gaining a new perspective on stressful situations.
- Building skills to manage your stress.
- Increasing self-awareness.
- Focusing on the present.
- Reducing negative emotions.
- Increasing imagination and creativity.
- Increasing patience and tolerance.
- Lowering resting heart rate.
- Lowering resting blood pressure.
- Improving sleep quality.

Meditation induces our rest and digest responses, which are the opposite bodies to fight or flight responses, and you can see why it such a useful tool for us to use with all these benefits.

I completed my meditation teacher training in late summer of 2021 and ran a few taster courses with my colleagues and a couple of one-to-one sessions. Something was telling me I needed to focus on myself, though, so I've parked the instruction thing for now, although I have one of my "knowings" I will be using it again in the future to heal other people.

My practice has deepened and changed. The things I listed are related to the western benefits of meditation, however, there's also our spiritual side that develops with constant practice, meaning I have a deeper connection to who I am, other people and the universe.

Some other developments are:

- I can drop into meditation with my eyes open.
- I don't need a quiet, dark room to practise (although it is preferable).
- I can feel when my heart and mind are in coherence.
- I've found out who I am versus who I thought I was.

I'll explain what I mean by the last two points.

What is heart and mind coherence? This is when the heart communicates with your brain and they both synchronise their information exchange. I've put the heart first as it informs the brain how to function more than the brain does to the heart. Most people would think it would be the other way round but, when people say listen to your heart, it's not without reason, it knows best.

The heart-brain coherence is a state of oneness between your mind, body and spirit. This allows you to be more present and can heal your body. When I am in this state it feels like my heart has expanded to a circle twelve inches in diameter, there's a warm glowing feeling around the heart area and the front of my forehead tingles. I feel deeply peaceful and the best way to describe it is that feeling you have when you are about to fall asleep. Although, instead of lasting two minutes, it lasts for as long as I remain in the meditative state, which for me is normally between twenty to forty-five minutes.

Who I am versus who I thought I was. I thought I was my thoughts and the labels given to me: a husband, father, son, employee, friend, relation, male and many other things. After practising meditation and studying with teachers well in advance of my understanding, I now feel the essence of who I am is none of these things. These are part of the movie of life that my physical body acts in, but the screen that the movie is displayed on is who I am, this one step back from the content of experience. The movie and screen analogy I picked up from Rupert Spira, who is a meditation instructor, philosopher and artist I have learned a lot from.

I am the awareness that experiences thoughts, feelings, perceptions and sensations, and I respond to the labels I have been given but they do not define me.

When we are born, we have no labels or understanding of the world, yet we are aware. Our experiences, thoughts, feelings, perceptions and sensations constantly change, so we can't be them. Even the cells in our body die and then are replaced, so our core being can't be that.

The awareness I had as a child is the same one I had when I was eighteen, and the same one I have now, it is the only thing that is unchanged in my life. It doesn't care what I do, there's is no judgement or praise from it and it's peaceful when I sit with it.

Awareness or consciousness is the primary thing we are; without it, there is nothing to experience. If you bump your head and forgot all that you were, you'd still be you and our default operating system is awareness or consciousness.

It's not: I think, therefore I am.

It's: I am, therefore I think.

Or, in other words, because I am aware, I can think.

Mind chatter does not prove your existence, awareness does – well, sort of.

If you took everything physical away from the known universe, what would be left? The space that the matter occupied. If matter ceased to exist, the container of existence would still exist, so matter cannot be primary.

The world appears the way it does to us because of the equipment we have; eyes, ears, taste and touch. It would look different if you were a cat or a fly. All these realities – human, cat and fly – are correct all at once. We've only ever seen our version and others define their existence as like our own, so through consensus it leads us to believe it to be the only reality.

The world is an illusion but is also real. People misunderstand the word illusion, thinking it means not real, but it doesn't, it means not as it seems. I wish I could take credit for these understandings, but I am only a novice on this path, and we all need to start somewhere. It can sometimes be difficult to grasp these concepts, so finding an expert teacher to start with is key (something I'm not). Once you've been taught some concepts, it's time to drive your own car of self-discovery, which is where the fun begins.

I know a man who fits the bill as an expert, and this is where I found some of my teachings on the subject. His name is Rupert Spira. Rupert teaches the direct path, also known as Kashmir Shaivism (it sounds fancy but don't let that put you off). If this sort of thing interests you, you can find hours of Rupert's talks on YouTube or his website[3].

My favourite Rupert quote is: "There are three people sitting on the sofa looking at a TV, one person sees a landscape, one person sees a movie, the other sees a screen. They are all looking at the same thing, but the way they see dictates what they see."

I found Rupert's work helpful on changing my view from the person I thought I was into who I now know I am at primary state, which is awareness. It was a difficult road to trek down and took many hours of listening and relistening to the teachings before I got a basic understanding of it. It doesn't make it any less rewarding, though, as learning things that are easy is not as fun as a challenge is.

How Can You Get Started with Meditation?

There are always local groups to attend and online events. If you'd like to brush up on your skills before joining a group, then I would suggest the Calm or Insight timer apps. It's better to do short meditations to start with, five minutes is fine, but frequency is more important than duration. So,

---

3   www.rupertspira.com

keep them short and do five minutes a day; we can all find five minutes, can't we?

There are a million diverse types of meditation and it's all about finding the correct one for you. I love doing body scan and breath-focused meditations but struggle with visualisation ones, although I'm now better than when I started with them. Try as many as you can and you'll find one that works.

The most common thing I hear is, "I can't do it, my mind is too busy." That's a sure sign that meditation would be good for you. Don't be put off if your mind starts chattering, everybody's mind does; it's like training a dog to sit, repetition will show results. It's not about having no thoughts, it's about coming back to your practice when thoughts enter your head. Eventually, you will start to see the benefits I described; it just takes time and time is all we have!

As well as Rupert, I found the work of Joe Dispenza. They are two contrasting styles of teacher but equally as extraordinary. Joe Dispenza is a medical doctor and brings a lot of science to the art of meditation with some remarkable results of healing people. I would recommend looking into his work and the many podcasts he's been on. Joe brings the power of the mind to the masses; he reveals the science behind the body and mind's ability to heal itself even when conventional medicine said it was impossible. Joe healed himself from a bad spinal injury in twelve weeks and now teaches others not only how to heal themselves but how to lead the life they want to.

Joe has an online progressive course on his website,[4] which I undertook. He has authored many books; my two favourites are *You Are the Placebo* and *Breaking the Habit of Being Yourself*.

Joe runs weeklong retreats around the planet; attending one is on my to do list (it's a lengthy list).

What are you waiting for? Get your zen on!

---

4   www.drjoedispenza.com

CHAPTER 20

Yoga, Breathwork and Healing the Inner Child

D o you ever wonder why it is that when you see a beautiful landscape you become emotional? It's because, in that moment, the landscape disconnects you from the thinking mind and shows you who you really are. When we see beauty, we see our true nature reflected to us; we are the landscape, and the landscape is us. It's that recognition that sparks the emotion.

It's the same situation as I discussed in chapter seventeen where your partner reflects the love in you. Your partner reflects love, nature reflects awe and beauty, they are in essence the same energy.

When I started yoga, I didn't think for a minute that the statement above would be one of the side effects of doing this practice, but internal insights and connection to the world around me grew within me. For a long time, it wasn't this, it was just exercise. A lot of the instruction out there nowadays is just that, a form of exercise with no spiritual side. There's nothing wrong with that, exercise isn't a bad thing, but for me, I thought I may as well just go to the gym or an aerobics class.

That was until I found Kundalini yoga in January 2021. Even then, this was a slow burner, but I'll say it again, the more you practise things, the more things develop. I started my practice with my teacher Jo McCoy. Jo is based in North Berwick not far from where I live. From the outset, she has been kind and encouraging in my practice with her.

The first eighteen months, I was still in my head, thinking, *Am I doing it correctly? I can't do this pose, God my arms and legs hurt*, etc. After that, though, something clicked, and I started to relax more. On more than one occasion, I was reduced to tears at the end of the practice; not in a bad way, but I felt a release of energy or deep connection to the source as I call it.

If you'd told me a few years earlier that I would be doing yoga and meditation regularly, I would have thought you were mad. But here I am and I'm loving it! It demonstrates to me that even if you think you won't like it, why not try new things, as you never know where it will lead.

I now get up at 5am each morning and have a morning routine, which includes meditation, yoga and breathwork. Doing this has given me a sense of community and commitment. It has really deepened my practice and connection to others. There are so many distinct types of yoga that if you try one and don't like it, try another, at least try a few. It's great for your life and I find it's like a magnet that attracts positive things into your life. It's good for your body, good for your mind, good for your heart and good for the collective human race. It teaches you to raise your vibration, which in turn helps the collective.

There are loads of classes in the cities and if you live more remotely there are millions of online offerings. Even if you think it's not for you, at least give it a go first, then decide; you may, like me, learn to love it.

Breathwork is part of my Kundalini yoga, but I've also studied various modalities of it as a standalone practice. I started with the Wim Hoff method but preferred Owaken Breathwork. I did adopt the daily morning cold showers from Wim Hoff, though. You don't need to have long showers, just start off at ten seconds and increase it incrementally to a couple of minutes. The first thing you'll notice if you do cold showers is how much they wake you up; it's a great jolt that I do every morning. It's been proven to be good for your mental health and reduce inflammation of bodily systems.

In a breathwork practice, you can use your breath in an activation way to boost your energy or use it to calm you down, just like in meditation. There are three main techniques that I use. The rest and restore breath is where you breathe in and out of your nose slowly. This kind of breathing activates your parasympathetic nervous system, aka the rest and digest system. It brings your body into alignment or homeostasis.

The next technique is a midway point, where you breathe in through your nose and out through your mouth. This provides a little more activation to your sympathetic system, aka fight or flight response.

Lastly, we can go full out and breathe in and out of our mouths for a fully activated effect. This one is useful if you want to go deeper quicker.

As well as breathing in and out, after a set number of breaths or duration of time, you hold your breath at certain points. The breath holds range in length up to as long as you can without gasping for air. Breath holds give you quite a high and can make some people a bit dizzy. After multiple rounds, you can reach a meditative state.

During some classes, once you are in the meditative state, the facilitator will give a guided meditation, which can be good if you want to release emotion tied to the past or visualise a future that you want for yourself.

I've done short fifteen-to-thirty-minute sessions with Owaken Breathwork where we focus on a topic that aligns with what is happening in our life at that time, like:

- Meet uncomfortable emotions.
- Breathe into your potential.
- Raise your self-worth.
- Release guilt with love.
- Boost your energy for the day.

The Owaken Breathwork team of Lukis Mac and Helle Weston are amazing. They have a website and an app that has lots of differently aligned shortish sessions. It is a subscription-based service, but it works out under £1 a day for a monthly subscription.

Periodically, they also do live events that last five hours and take a deeper dive aligned to healing. These can be great for releasing pent-up emotion or energy. When I've done these classes, I've always felt amazing afterwards.

Breathwork gets you into that same alpha brainwave state that meditation does, but I find it more useful to use breathwork to accept and release difficult emotions. I can also tap into my intuition when I'm looking for answers using this method.

I do a mixture of personal practice, in-person group work and online guided. I found with yoga and breathwork you need to find an instructor who resonates with you, so shop around until you find one that suits.

Inner Child

When I talked about sorting out our minds earlier in the book, I also meant the subconscious part. We behave, act, and react to people and situations using a default programme that we have built up over the years. The programme lives in the subconscious, and throughout our childhood, we learn limiting bullshit that we believe about ourselves. *I can't, it's too hard, I'm stupid, they are better than me.*

As it's in the subconscious, you might be living your life in a happy place in your awakened state, but the default programme will pop up every so often. Learning to access this programme to change self-limiting beliefs can be an effective way to improve your overall mental well-being. We can't access the unconscious in everyday life, but with meditation, yoga and breathwork we can.

There are different interpretations of inner child work,

and this is my interpretation. If inner child sounds to woo for you then just call it unconscious mind reprogramming. If you could go back in time, give that younger self a hug, speak to them and release the negative comments that had been said to you, or you thought about yourself, you would, right? If you dissolve learned feelings and thoughts that still limit you decades later, isn't that a good thing?

As I learned, it's not a one and done practice – well, it wasn't for me. I had to repeatedly access and work through my shit before I saw results. To give you an example of how this default programme can affect your life, I'll tell you about an unconscious emotion I worked through.

I can honestly say I have never been happier in my life than I am now. I have a 100% secure relationship, yet I have a recurring dream several times per month where my wife Anneke has left me and, worse still, when I go to other people to speak to them, they all shun me.

After sitting with this for a while, it was clear to me that, somewhere in my subconscious, I have a deep-rooted fear of being alone. The opposite of my conscious day-to-day wakened life.

This is where using breathwork and meditation helped me access the alpha brainwave state and, in turn, access my subconscious. During this, I visualise my younger self and try to see what comes up. My youngest memories came to mind where I pictured myself in a cot crying in the darkness. I also have a vivid memory of my first days at nursery crying at the window as my mum left to go to work.

A lot of kids go through separation anxiety when going to school or nursery for the first time and it's part of life. You can't be with your parents all the time when you are little, we need to socialise with other children. But it must have influenced me to give me a learned fear of being alone and, given these are only two of the three memories I have up to the age of three, they must have affected me deeply. The early thoughts and beliefs about ourselves are important, as these mould the way we see and behave in the world.

Through meditation and breathwork, you can go back and remould the negative sculpture you have of yourself or situations and create a new design more aligned to the person you want to be.

Once in a meditative state, we ask ourselves the question: what age child wants to show up and speak to me? We try to picture ourselves at that age. We then ask our younger self what limiting belief they wish to talk about. You often find it's *I'm not enough, I'm a failure, I'm unlovable, I'm lonely, or I'm scared*. For me, it was that he was alone. We first must acknowledge the feeling that's being brought forward, before releasing the limiting feeling or thought. I did this by reassuring the younger version of myself that I was there to protect him and it was time to let this go. You may need to visit this space several times, depending on how many limiting beliefs you have and how ingrained they are, but I found it a major source of healing.

When doing this meditation, a five-year-old me turned up and I told him how successful in life he had become and how happy he was as a grown-up. On my last visualisation of my younger self, which happened during a yoga session and wasn't planned, I pictured young me skipping about singing as he now knows that he can never be alone if he is connected to his heart. I came out of this feeling about ten stone lighter.

I realised by doing change work that there are parts of me shouting, *Wahoo! Let's go, we love it.* But there is also that young part of me saying, *If you put this book out there, do that new thing, stop drinking, people will laugh and ridicule you. Stay where you are, it's safe here.*

When you are on the path of change, expect this. There will be resistance. This was my survival mode saying, *Stay under the radar; no one can hurt you if they can't see you.* This is how I had stayed safe in the past, but to become the person I want to be, I have to feel compassion for that view. I also had to work with it every day until it was released, and I became one step closer to the person aligned to the path I'm running down.

You will be surprised how many times people come out of these meditations with tears due to releasing hurt or feeling joy. Our minds don't differentiate between a thought and reality. Don't believe me? Think of a time when you've worried about something that you had to do the next day, tossing and turning, not being able to get to sleep, how did that make you feel? But it wasn't real, was it? It hadn't happened yet, so why did you feel so apprehensive about the next day? Because your brain doesn't know the difference between now and the future. This works with the past too. You can reframe a negative thought or feeling of the past to something more positive. It's just one of the ways we can heal our brokenness and can be great if you have trauma as a child. However trivial you think the trauma is as an adult, a child sees it differently.

Help the little you as though they were your son or daughter; and in some ways, they are.

CHAPTER 21

Podcasts, Podcasts, Podcasts

This is a short chapter but an important one. If you are looking for personal development, then inspiration and guidance is the fuel for that fire. I found this in the form of listening to and learning from others, people who had been through a lot tougher situations than I had, experts who had studied techniques and life hacks.

It's been proven in studies that watching mainstream media can have a detrimental effect on your mental health due to the amount and frequency of negativity they spout. Not to mention the known negative effect of spending too much time on platforms like Twitter or Facebook, which promote controversy.

Well, guess what, that works in reverse! Thank God for the duality of the world. That's right, if you listen to positive media, it will improve your mental health. The biggest source of this that I've found is podcasts, and the best bit is there's loads of free content on sites such as YouTube and Spotify. I know, I say that a lot, right? But there are people who think YouTube is for music and cat videos, but they have some amazingly useful guidance.

I first got into podcasts after a trip to the doctor. I had been for an appointment about an issue I was having with pain in my foot. He recommended some treatment but also said I should listen to a podcast by Dr Rangan Chatterjee. I listened to the recommended podcast, then I came across another of Dr Chatterjee's podcasts with John McAvoy, who as a young man was a serious criminal. He turned his life around by focusing his skills on sporting achievement. I was left totally inspired by this guy. I urge you to listen to his story; from sitting in his cell in a maximum-security prison, he had an epiphany that he wanted to change. He went on to become a top endurance athlete with world records to his name – world records, I may add, that he broke whilst in jail. It made me think if John can do this from his position, then I've no excuse. If I wanted to change then it was up to me and 100% possible.

I read John's book, then before I knew it, I had branched out, finding new podcasts and new books. I started listening to podcasts daily, I'd look for podcasts of inspiring stories or how to motivate myself, how to reframe my thinking, meditations, breathwork, just anything that was of a positive nature and may help me develop the skills I have. To this day, I still listen to podcasts every day.

Try finding something that inspires you. Inspiration is something that sparks you into life, a light-bulb moment, a desire to change, a moment of clarity. It can be all you need to make that change happen.

Here are some people to check out. Some of these

people may be deemed controversial. I don't agree with all they say, but I do agree with at least some of their views. I think it's important in this day and age of social cancellation and avoidance of opposing views that we take a balanced approach and listen to those who you don't or only partially agree with and debate them. Just because I strongly disagree with you on one point, it does not mean you don't have a valid standpoint. This is where progress is made, instead of the 'my way or the highway' approach. Or, even worse, think we need to constantly check the current accepted narrative in case someone, somewhere, may take offence.

- Peter Crone
- Eckhart Tolle
- Rupert Spira
- Russel Brand
- Lex Fridman
- Heal
- Gerry Murphy
- Jordan Peterson
- Joe Rogan
- Aubrey Marcus
- Alister Gray (mindful coaching)
- Fern Cotton
- Dr Rangan Chatterjee
- Jay Shetty
- Alan Neachell
- Blu
- Chris Williamson

- Duncan Trussell
- Rich Roll
- Amrit Nam
- John Vervaeke

I also cut out my intake of the news. In fact, I watch so many podcasts and have other interests now that my daily slouch on the couch to watch TV has dramatically dropped. I also stopped using Twitter and Facebook and it made such a difference to my head space.

If you fill your head with negativity, is it any wonder it has a harmful effect on you? So don't do it, fill it full of positivity. If you keep on looking, you will find someone that resonates with you and take notes or journal on what they say and how you can apply it to your life.

In the next chapter, we discuss the change I made that had the biggest impact. Why? Because it brought all the other changes together and gave me more time to do the things I wanted to do.

CHAPTER 22

The Drunken Mun-key

(Getting Aff It)

I suppose the first thing I need to do for the people reading this book who are not from Scotland is provide a definition of "aff it". Those who are from Scotland will surely understand the term, if not having used it in some form themselves.

"Aff it" is a Scottish term meaning "off it". Now, to complicate things, as we Scots like to do, it has more than one meaning. I'll use it in a few sentences in Scots and then explain it in plain – if somewhat comedic – English.

1. The guy over there is aff it = that man over there is extremely inebriated or high on drugs.
2. I'm aff it the day = I don't wish to partake in any further consumption of alcohol, I drank too much last night and the thought of it makes me feel rather nauseous.
3. I'm aff it = I no longer drink or take drugs as I have had enough of the hangovers and come downs to last me three lifetimes. This time I mean it for good. (Normally a lie, but some of us do indeed stay aff it.)

4. He's aff it = That man is not right in head.

I think I have said or been all these definitions at some point in my life, but this chapter is about how and why I gave up the booze for good.

I need to be clear: I have no issue with anybody who does drink, and I don't avoid situations that involve the consumption of it. I still go to the pub, go out for meals, go to the football, I just don't booze when I'm doing these things.

Stopping drinking has been part of my personal development and I started giving up almost three years ago. It's like learning to drive a car, you need practice and stall a few times. This chapter is not meant to be a lecture on the demon drink. I'm not going to get on a pulpit and condemn you to hell if you do partake in a sherry or two. I just think it's important to discuss my relationship with alcohol, and how it changed over the years. It might help someone in the same boat, but if you think it's not for you then you can always skip the chapter. (I'll know if you have, though, and you'll go on the naughty list!)

A lot of people reading this will still like a drop of the amber nectar, mummy's relax water, the hooch, fire water, wah-wah juice, the devil's piss, aka alcohol. But I can't see me ever drinking again. For me, there are too many benefits to give up and so much shit I don't have to deal with anymore. But forever is a long time, so let's just say, at this point in time, I have no intention of drinking alcohol again.

(Don't worry I won't be having a drink to celebrate publishing my book, well, perhaps a cup of tea.)

I, like most people in Scotland, started drinking before the legal age of eighteen. By the time I was eighteen, I was drinking on average twice per week. I could spring out of bed after a night out and the hangovers weren't that bad.

By the time I was in my mid-twenties, I was drinking on average three times per week. It was never just two pints then going home, I was always last out and drinking until the money ran out or I was drunk as a skunk. A lot of the time, I was using it to block the emotional pain I had inside, or because I was bored and lonely. As I got older, the hangovers were also getting a tad worse, to say the least, meaning missing days at work, spending all day in my bed, doing and saying things I really didn't want to or mean.

This carried on into my mid-thirties. After counselling and getting at least some of my pain out of my head, the frequency of my boozing started to slow down, but the amount I consumed when I did go out did not. The aftereffects got worse too, the hangxiety after a night out troubled me and it lasted longer, sometimes two to three days. I was able to push through these hangovers a lot better, though, giving the appearance of nothing being out of sorts.

I had been given a promotion at work, which came with extra responsibilities. I also wanted to make something of my life. Although, as I discussed earlier in the book, I was using my fear of failure to propel me on to success, it was better than being a non-functioning, negative member of society, but far from ideal. So, with fear driving me, I never missed a day of work, even with bad hangovers.

After a night out drinking, I'd feel like I had shot someone in the face the night before. I'd think about all my earlier fuck-ups and torture myself with thinking about them over and over. Mostly, all I had ever done was speak shit for a few hours with my mates, I'd never shot anyone, that's for sure. I'd wake up, go through this mental torture and tell myself, *NEVER AGAIN*, which is another common saying in Scotland. However, the very next week I would start the cycle all over again.

I got married in 2017 when I was forty-four. By this time, I was only really drinking twice a month and sometimes would go a couple of months without. It did not stop the severe hangovers, though, when I did partake in a binge. My hangovers lasted three days every time by this point.

It's time to address two pearls of wisdom I would hear from others about my drinking habits when I discussed my issues. (As if I hadn't thought of them myself.)

1. Why don't you just give up drinking?

It's a good point. Why didn't I? Well, I didn't think I had it in me. I mean, it's everywhere, christenings, weddings, funerals, work nights out, football, let's face it, every social event includes drinking. All I had known was this, the two went hand in hand. I'd tell myself I was weak, it was too hard, and I couldn't do it, or so I thought. There are a million different excuses why you can't stop drinking, and I've thought of all of them.

You can stop, though, but not if you don't change the way you look at things. If you start off with *I can't, I'm missing out*, etc., you will be doomed to fail. A good tip I was told before giving up was to list all the reasons why you want to give up and keep them nearby. Then list all the positive things that will come from stopping. Even if it's just "no hangovers and I'll save money" to start with, you can add more as you progress. Believe me, there will be more that spring to mind the longer you stay sober. I get days of my life back, for example, not sitting on a sofa watching TV through the gaps in my fingers unable to move without feeling sick.

First things first, you need to change your view from *I'm giving up the booze* to > *I'm gaining XXXX back.*

If you are sitting there reading this, thinking, *It's okay for him to say that but he's not me*, then you're correct, I'm not you, but we share something in common. A voice inside our heads that doesn't want us to do difficult things, it likes the status quo (no, not the band) and doesn't want things to change. It's the same voice that stops you going to the gym, or makes you eat that extra cake. I'm here to tell you, that voice can get chucked right in the bin, you can train it to sit, just like your dog. It takes time but you can do it.

2. Why don't you just moderate?

This is a common and such a daft comment. Those who moderate already do so, but those who can't moderate

CAN'T MODERATE. The switch is off or on for me. I've tried but it just doesn't work. I end up enjoying two pints less than no pints as the craving has been switched on.

I've yet to meet someone who has gone from frequent binge drinking to just having one or two on a night out on a regular basis. You may be able to do it one, two or ten times in a row but eventually the little drunken monkey bastard will pop inside your mind, and you'll be on a session. I'm sure there will be some people out there who have done it, I've just not met them yet.

Moderation is something I tried on my first attempt to stop drinking. It worked for a while but was doomed to fail. On that note, let's look at where my first attempt to stop drinking started before eventually cracking that nut on the 27th of November, 2022.

The beginning of 2020 was the start of me coming home or finding me again. I had started my daily meditation practice and it was the first time I had seriously thought about giving up alcohol for good. There was a good but embarrassing story to go along with that. Sometimes when I drink a lot – and I mean a lot, perhaps a twelve-hour-plus binge – I need to pee during the night; who wouldn't? It's even worse now I'm turning fifty. But I do not always make it to the bathroom. You know where this is going, don't you? You see, I am not fully awake, and I go sleepwalking, but with peeing involved. It's happened four times in my life that I'm aware of and here in their full glory they are:

- Gone to pee on my mate's living room table only for another mate to stop me before full flow.

- Made it to the bathroom in a friend's house only to pee in the bath when there was a good toilet right beside it.
- Peed on my shoes in the corner of the room (didn't notice that until I went to put them on).

Now, I did wonder whether to include this, as it's not something I'm proud of, and now I'm telling you all about it. But do you know what? I thought fuck it, I don't care what people think, that's their judgement and not my business. This book was always going to push me out of my comfort zone and it's the truth, so I'm just telling it like it was.

The last time it happened, it was March 2020. I was in Newcastle seeing my long-time unofficial brother Mason. We met at a rave in 1992 and Mason was my best man twenty-five years later when I got married in 2017. Our friendship might have been borne out of getting out of our heads, but there was more to it than that. However, we did still go on a drinking sesh most times we met.

The meeting of March 2020 was no different and turned into a messy affair. We went out all day binge drinking, got back to Mason's house, stayed up until 4am boozing and went to bed. I woke up at 8:30am and realised this time I hadn't made it to the toilet or a corner of a room. I mean WTF, I'm forty-seven-year-old man, it was time to get a fucking grip on my life choices.

I came back and said, "That's it, I'm done." A few weeks later, when the UK went into lockdown and everybody got out the booze, I was on my sober as fuck train! For six months, I didn't touch a drop. I found it easy, as all the bars were closed due to lockdown and there were no social engagements going on. I could have had a drink in the house, but I was determined I was done with it.

There was one problem, though. I was doing this to prove to myself I didn't need drink in my life. However, in the back of my mind, I knew this was not forever. I still wanted to drink (at some point), believing I could moderate, but was using my willpower to achieve it. The problem was willpower runs out.

Six months later, some lockdown restrictions were lifted, and people were allowed to visit your house again. For that part of me that wanted to drink, this was the excuse it needed. I hadn't seen my parents in months, the weather was nice, let's have a BBQ and allow myself to drink, just once, of course.

I had the BBQ, got really drunk and woke up the next day with a huge hangover. I then proceeded to tell myself that it was okay and all I needed to do was only drink on big occasions and this was certainly a big occasion.

The next big occasion happened three months after the BBQ and, in between, I'd been to a few social gatherings where alcohol was the order of the day, but I just had alcohol-free beers, which gave me further evidence that I could moderate the frequency of boozy days at least.

How long do you think that lasted? Well, I can't remember the exact date, but it was not long after. I just started falling into the trap of justifying drinking every time I was out, as they all became "big occasions":

- Meet with a friend I've not seen in ages (better have a drink).
- It's the football, after all (better have a drink).
- It's a wedding (better have a drink).
- It's a blah blah blah (better have a drink).

So, there I was at the end of 2021 back to drinking on every social occasion. This lasted until November 2022 when I woke up with the standard hangover and thought, *That's it, I'm done! I'm not drinking again*. There was no drama, I hadn't done or said anything bad, I hadn't even sleep-peed. There was just something in me that changed. I wasn't proving a point this time; I just didn't want to drink anymore.

I've seen so many positives in my life that outweigh the few hours of being tanked up. This wasn't something I was tracking the last time round. I get up at 5am every day to do meditation and yoga, I'm going out for 5km walks, I'm eating healthier, I felt a deeper connection to myself and others, I am meeting new people and doing new activities, I've written this book and I'm in a real happy place in life.

I'd traded that for bad anxiety, making an idiot of myself, wasting days of my life because I couldn't function, saying things I didn't mean, eating unhealthily, placing limiting beliefs on myself and poor sleep cycles.

It wasn't just this one thing that changed my life, it was the culmination of doing all the other me work. Stopping drinking just helped all the other positive changes seem even better. One step at a time up the mountain. But this was one of the bigger changes for me, as I honestly believed

I'd never do it. But why on earth would I want to go back now?

What really helped me was my inspirational wife Anneke. She'd given up booze eighteen months before I completely stopped. I'd seen the positive change it had made in her life. She'd never once said to me that I should stop, as she knew it wouldn't help and it was my choice. I got there in my own time and my own way.

Anneke had joined an app called Dryy, which is run by Andy Ramage, Matt Pink and Chrystal Day, who are life coaches and general cheerleaders for those on the app. It is designed for people who are sober curious or are determined to make the change. There are lots of people who are years in to their sober journey who cheer and help those at the start of theirs. There are meet ups and activities in various cities, so you can meet other like-minded people, webinars, coaching classes and sober holidays.

There are subscription-based groups if you want to take a deeper dive. I joined one called Off the Sesh, which is for men only. I found it a major help to talk to lads who were just the same as me and had similar relationship issues with booze. I'm also on another subgroup called Mind, which is coaching on all areas of your life. There's even coaching training if you want to do that. I would recommend anyone who wants to give up drinking alcohol to give this app a go, there's lots of great personal development information on there.

One caveat, though: the app is not for chemically dependent addicts. This is made clear from the start. It's not a replacement for medical advice or rehab.

Now, me telling these stories might make you think, *I'm not as bad with the drink as you, Steve, so I'm okay.* That might be true, but there's a little test you can do. Listening to your feelings, when you think about you and drinking, is there a part that knows *I wish it wasn't this way*? Then you have two options: make the change or carry on with the same results.

I guarantee that if there were two versions of you living the same life, one who drank alcohol and one who didn't, the one who didn't would out-perform the one who did. By performance, I mean in all areas, work, family, health, connection to yourself and others, sleep, workouts, emotional well-being and happiness, the thing we all want.

If you feel you don't have an issue with drink in your life then bash on, there's nothing to worry about! If you think, *I'd really like to, but I don't know how*, then there is an out.

Over and above the Dryy app, there are the following books that might help:
- Andy Ramage: *The 28 Day Alcohol-Free Challenge* and *Let's Do This*
- Matt Pink: *Better Me, Better You*
- Annie Gracie: *The Naked Mind*

You also might want to check out the *Menace to Sobriety* podcast with Daniel O'Reilly. This one change in my life, threw me miles down the personal growth path and that's when things really began to ramp up.

CHAPTER 23

Going to Workshops and Events

Flare Festival

O nce I had given up drinking alcohol, it was like lighting the touchpaper of enthusiasm. I wanted to get involved in as many new things as possible. The Dryy app had organised a meet up in Edinburgh and Glasgow. People from the app could meet up, go for a healthy walk, then connect through having a coffee afterwards. From these two meet ups, I have met loads of new friends who are also on the going sober journey. One of them mentioned a one-day well-being festival in Edinburgh that was coming up called Flare.

Both Anneke and I decided to go along to Flare, as the classes on offer looked good, and boy, I'm glad we did. The festival was made up of various workshops going on in many different rooms from 10am to 7pm. Two of these stood out for me. The first was with Life Force Exclusive hosted by Lynette Gray and Natalie Smith. Lynette and Natalie both told their stories of what had brought them to do what they do now, which is coaching and helping people, amongst other things. Both these woman had inspiring stories to tell, and it made me think, "I want to do that."

We moved on to do some movement through dance, something I could tell Lynette was passionate about, then we did a bit of meditation and journalling. What came through for me was that it was time for me to finish writing this book. I had started it a while before sorting out my limiting beliefs but parked it, thinking it wouldn't be good enough. Now I felt I did have something to say.

At the end of the workshop, I went up to thank Lynette and Natalie. I spoke to Natalie to say I had enjoyed the workshop and it had given me the kick up the bum I needed. Lynette joined us and asked me what I had taken from the workshop. I said I was going to finish my book, with the hope that it may help someone.

I will always remember Lynette's response: "It's not 'may help someone'; it's 'will help someone'."

Even then, there was a part of me that didn't want to be so confident in my words. I thanked Lynette for that reframing and off I went to the next class.

Now, if I had not stopped drinking, I wouldn't have gone on the Dryy walking event, I wouldn't have known about Flare Festival, I wouldn't have met Lynette and Natalie and you would not be reading this book as it would have remained unfinished.

It's funny how one decision when aligned to your greater good can lead to all this. Now I'm not saying you need to stop drinking; I'm saying making decisions in alignment with your calling will tend to produce outcomes like this. So, a big thank you Lynette and Natalie, a copy of the book will be on its way to you when it comes out.

Strangely enough, later that day, I attended another class with Lynette's brother Alister Gray. Alister led a great meditation called awakening love, which dovetailed into the self-enquiry work I had been doing through my own meditation practice.

It also turns out that Alister runs Mindful Talent as a coach, which also has courses where you can train to be a coach. This is something I had wanted to do but was looking for a company that came at things with a spiritual angle built into the coaching.

BINGO! Mindful Talent fit the bill. I completed their insight course, which I found amazing, and I'm doing further coaching accreditation later in 2023. Who knows, I may even work with you in future if you need some life coaching to achieve the dream you always wanted or if you need a prod to make a change.

One decision opened both these doors that day and this is the power of trying out new interests and habits.

CHAPTER 24

The Importance of Community

I t wasn't until January 2023 that I found the importance of community. I didn't even know it was something I wanted; it was just a happy by-product of taking up so many new pursuits.

I am coming up for fifty and I have great long-time friends, I just didn't see them that often. This is the norm as you get older, everybody is so busy doing their own thing that the meet ups are infrequent. It wasn't until I started attending daily morning yoga or groups for lads who want to stop drinking or going to retreats that I gained a real sense of community and saw the immense value in it.

Some of these people I met in person and some were just online, but we had common interests. In some of these groups, I could see I was helping people, and in turn, they were helping me. This could be with advice or clarity on something I was having an issue with.

I'd forgotten what it felt like to belong. I had it in my raving days where we were all on the same mission of partying and pushing back against society. This time round, it was more about connection, sharing our experiences and helping people who were struggling, or even just in need of an ear to rant at.

I'd heard lots of the well-being gurus on podcasts talking about our need for community, but I never really took it on board. As humans, we are social animals, we are not meant to be alone, we are meant to forge connections to give us a sense of security. If we are lucky, we have strong family connections and a few good friends. Sadly, this is not everybody's reality and for those people who fit into this category with no sense of connection, life can be miserable.

There is a loneliness epidemic in the UK, to the point that we even appointed a minister in government to tackle the problem. How is it even possible that we have let the country get to the point of needing a loneliness minister?

Loneliness is something that's within our control and connection is the solution. By attending classes and finding interests, you will start to gain that sense of community and bond with people. I appreciate some people are shy but all the work we do should push us out of our comfort zone or we'll not grow. If you are shy, go to a class with a friend or work colleague or even join online classes to start with (in-person classes are always better, though).

Here's how I created a wider community in 2023. I'm hoping you'll find some inspiration.

Dryy App

I talked about the Dryy app in previous chapters, but it was probably the most important decision I made in finding community again. The people I met opened a new network of contacts who were facilitating or attending events that helped in my personal development. Through the Dryy app, I received some coaching, met like-minded lads who were sober, went on healthy walks, went axe throwing, went out for lunches and attended talks.

This led me to some great life-changing experiences, making new connections and friendships. So, let's look at the connection highlight for me in 2023.

Men's Circle (Day Workshop)

On the 18th of March 2023, I attended a workshop designed for men, a men's circle if you will. This retreat was run by David Millar from Mantra Menswork and Rory Lamont from Caim Retreat Centre.

I had worked with Rory before at his retreat centre, which he runs with his partner Shannon. The work I had done with Rory and Alan Wilson of You Revolution at Caim happened a few weeks before the men's circle event and it was life changing for me. I came away with a purpose and I let go of some of the limiting beliefs I'd held about myself. The teachings I learned that day are of a personal, sacred nature, so I'm sorry folks, this I won't be sharing; we all have boundaries and that's one of mine. All I can say is I am eternally grateful to Alan, Rory, Shannon, Mike and all the brothers who attended that day.

I had booked the men's circle prior to the Caim retreat with the intention of learning new things. After the work with Rory, Alan and Mike, I had an additional intention, which was to be of service to others. If my words or actions help one person, then it will have been a good day. This is something I hope to carry forward every day.

As this space is also sacred and confidential, I can only share my views and thoughts of the day. David started proceedings outlining the schedule and discussed why it is important that men start to connect. Being open about our feelings and how awareness of and working with our guiding energies can make us better men. We then moved on to doing an activating breathwork session. These sessions can be profoundly cathartic, where emotional wounds are healed and blocked energy released. This session was no different. From a personal point, an overwhelming feeling of joy came over me. I burst into tears as I felt a wave and vibration across my body. I was in good company as all around I could hear tears and wailing; there was something deeply primal about some of those noises.

After some integration time, we then moved on to a grounding meditation, which brought our mind and heart into coherence. This was to bring us back into our bodies before we moved on to working with David.

David explained we'd be working with the Jungian masculine archetypes, which are the magician, the lover, the king and the warrior. These energies can manifest themselves in a light (mature) or dark way (immature). The aim for me was to understand how these can come forth, in both ourselves, and in other men. This would enable me to more fully understand myself and others and develop as a man.

After only working with these concepts for one day, I'm obviously no expert, but I found this work interesting. David devised exercises that helped us work with each archetype in turn. As these may be David's intellectual property, I won't go into detail, but let's just say they did push me out of my comfort zone and revealed to me what I need to work on to improve as a man. I need to take my foot off the gas a little, I need to let go of something from my past that I had thought I'd already dealt with, but I obviously haven't. See, I am still *Imprfct* after all, even with the work I've done.

This highlighted to me the importance of the gathering of men, where we can bring forth our issues, hopes and dreams and seek the guidance of other men without fear of judgement or ridicule. These are the places of acceptance and of great healing that this planet needs.

The same can be said for the female energies of this world. There are women's circles springing up everywhere. We can develop as men and women in our own circles and then come together in a shared space, stronger and more resilient. We must do what needs to be done and together we can shift the planet to the light.

CHAPTER 25

The Snowball Effect

(Take your time)

I would like to point out the snowball effect of positive change. Once you start on this road of positivity, you'll find that one interest or pursuit leads on to another and, before you know it, you'll have loads of great new interests in your life.

I started to read and listen to personal development information, I worked on reframing my mind, I took up meditation, I found yoga, I found breathwork, I stopped drinking, I found out who I was and connected to others easier, I went to wellness festivals, I went to a retreat, I published my book. I am now looking into my nutrition and after that I will be looking to lift heavy things to improve my strength.

After that, who knows, another load of experiences and another book, becoming a coach and helping others. These are all possibilities I have in front of me now, which I didn't have prior to starting down the path of change in March 2020.

But a word of caution: it's important not to overload yourself. Focus on one thing at a time so as not to spread yourself too thin. All these things I've tried happened over several years; if I'd tried to start them all at once, I'd have blown a circuit. I also tried some things that didn't resonate with me, so I dropped them. Don't do something because you think you must, do it because you want to and enjoy it. (Except breathing and eating, of course.)

Think of what some people do in January. They start going to the gym, cut out junk food, stop smoking and give up alcohol for the month. If you do all three at once, your body/mind won't cope, and you'd be lucky to keep it going for six weeks, never mind forever.

Pick one thing to focus on, let it become part of who you are over a couple of months, then move on to the next thing. You won't need as much mind energy to keep up the first activity you started as it will already be part of you.

I read a great book on motivation and change that really helped me with this called *Let's Do This* by Andy Ramage, which has these concepts in it. I bought this after listening to him on Dr Chatterjee's podcast. In the podcast, Andy discussed his book, which describes how to build motivation and, more importantly, how to keep it going. Andy believes gaining motivation and keeping it going need to be tackled in two separate ways, as they are different beasts.

Reading Andy's book gave me an understanding of what it would take for me to achieve the things I wanted to achieve; I just needed to apply these to my life. The book gives you a background of how your mind works when setting goals and provides a twenty-eight-day process to follow. In short, it helps you ingrain positive habits into your identity, which makes it easier than having to resist negative habits through willpower alone.

CHAPTER 26

Some Final Words

Why did I go for *Imprfct* instead of imperfect?

A few reasons, really. *Imprfct* was one of the designs I used on the T-shirts I made in India when I was living as a beach bum. It was my most popular creation and it would make people do a double take.

The second reason is I think it's wrong to perfectly spell imperfect. I mean, it can't be imperfect if it's spelt perfectly. It goes against the word's nature and what the word stands for. I assume when you read *Imprfct* you knew the word that I was referring to, so what's the hassle, I wrote, you understood, that's communication, baby!

Lastly, given my challenges with language and my nature, it's a perfect word to describe me. Just like *Imprfct*, people understand me, but I'm not all there. Or maybe I am all there and I like playing the trickster sometimes – I'll let you decide.

Imprfct or imperfect? We all have subjective views of reality, none of which can be wholly defined as true or perfect. I recently listened to a presentation by American cognitive psychologist and popular science author Donald Hoffmann. In the lecture, Hoffmann discussed that the natural selection of our ancestors did not align with those who saw the truth of reality, but to those who saw the best fit of it. Basically, our brains can't handle the truth, so we see a lo-fi icon-based version of it. Maybe that's what we see when we take hallucinogenic substances, the truth? And perhaps why some can't handle it – the truth and the hallucinations – but some of us can!

If Hoffmann is correct, then the space and time that we and the universe occupy is only our cognitive representation of reality that best allows us to survive. It's not how things truly are and, if that's the case, maybe in the "real" version of reality, *Imprfct* is how it's spelt.

Interpretations and perceptions can have a big impact on your life in a positive and negative way; it's all an internal narrative. And as for other people's negative opinions on my views of the correct spelling? In the bin!

Are you confused? Good, welcome to my world.

The world we live in is an illusion in as much as no two being's physical realities, human or otherwise, can ever be the same. The thing we call life is just a culmination of stories that we tell ourselves and others, to define our physical self-identity. Although beyond this, there is the "I" of awareness, which is our true self.

These stories are mere perspectives, and if you don't like the physical identity you have, then learn to create a different one, or even better, live from a place beyond your identity labels. By shifting your perspective on life, it can be moulded into whatever you want it to be. It may not seem possible, but it is, it just takes a willingness to change and sometimes a little help is all that's needed.

If you don't take an interest in the story of you, then life will choose a story for you. The question to ask yourself is: do you want to be only an actor? Or do you want to be the actor, director and producer of the vast film of your life?

I've not led a rockstar lifestyle by any means, but compared to some, I've had some interesting challenges and situations happen to me (or is that *for* me?) and here I am, writing the final paragraphs of my book. The limited version of me that I was would never have had the courage to finish this book, but the person I chose to become did. It may not be a literary masterpiece, it may even be considered the ramblings of a mad man, but so what, that's not the point, it's my story. What's yours going to be? Limited or unlimited?

The Calling

It's time to take the first step in healing your brokenness, to get out there and find what brings you your mojo! Look for new interests that are aligned to positive values. It will be good for your well-being and create new healthy connections in your life, expanding the circle of friends you have.

It's time for you to step up and make a change, however small. You don't need to change the world; you only need to change you and that will change the world. Once you show a positive change, the benefits spread out like ripples from a pebble being dropped in a pond. First to those who are closest to you, then this will change the people in their life, it's an ever-expanding circle of light.

As humans, we have lost connection to the planet, we have lost connection to each other, we have lost connection to ourselves. There is a shift already in place on earth, the dark energy is receding as the light is sparked person by person.

Action is needed and if you feel the call to change yourself or to help others, listen to the quiet calling inside you, this is your soul speaking. Take the first step to change and, when you get knocked to the floor, get up and keep climbing that hill. There is a warrior in each of us, which only needs awakening; it's a hard path but it is where meaning is found. So, what can you do today?

I have felt my calling all my life. It was a feeling there was more to life than I was being told by the controlling forces within our society. At first, I tried to find it in people, places, substances and things. Then in the years 2020 to 2023, I slowly realised it was a lot closer to home. It was a connection to myself, the planet, my community and the source, this was what I was looking for. The men's day retreat and the people and conversations I had there I found life changing.

If you do not feel a calling or if these words do not resonate with you, then there is no need to read past this paragraph, but know this: there is a quickening happening and the forces of light are finding each other. There are peaceful warriors fighting a cause for you, and your children, and your children's children's future. You'll recognise these brothers and sisters easily as their words will resonate with truth, even if it goes against the accepted narrative; their energy is ferocious, but kind. These are the people looking to shift the planet's dark energy back into the light. These are the people who live in service of others and do not give up.

If you are reading this paragraph, then perhaps the words of "there must be more to life than this" do resonate with you. You may be aware that what we are being told in the worlds of politics, health, finance and food do not ring true.

Ask yourself the question: what can I do to improve my life? The better choices you make, the better your life will become. Do the things that are hard, as this is how steel is made, and they will forge a stronger you. Through struggle, the greatest things are achieved; the shoot of a tree bursting through the ground, the birth of a child, turning negative habits into positive. These struggles all come with pain, but on the other side of that pain is the meaning you are seeking.

Seek the truth and the people who speak it, find your people, we are out there. Help shift the planet's future, join us, as we are the warriors of the light! And through the actions of truth, ferocious energy and kindness, you will know us. We love you regardless of whether you are enemy or friend, but we have little time for controlling powers and our unity gives us strength.

Take heed of what you think, eat, do and even say. The words that we use are part of the fifth element of sound. Words have a similar energy to music and are a powerful force. How you use your words can inspire or cause harm. Your use of words cannot only cause inspiration and harm to others, but they can also be a positive or negative driving force towards yourself.

Take time before believing the thoughts, words, or ideas you have of yourself. They may not be a truth or aligned to your highest good, in fact frequently they are far from aligned. Even after much focus and awareness on this concept, I still must be vigilant, but when I mess up – and I do – I forgive myself. Why? Because I know I'm *IMPRFCT* and that's okay!

It is time for this part of my story to end, but the mission is far from complete. I hope you enjoyed my words and have found the inspiration you need to become the person you know you can be. I may even see some of you out in the well-being community and I look forward to hearing your story.

If you'd like to connect with me, you can do so in several ways.

Personal: @imprfct_stevedavie – This will just be pictures and stories of me doing what I do, out and about in nature.

Business: @imprfct_healistic_coaching – This account will be for people who want to work with me in a coaching capacity. This will be launching towards the end of 2023 / start of 2024.

Substack: www.imprfct.substack.com – I write short pieces here, which are sometimes comedic, sometimes serious. It's generally whatever's kicking around my head that week.

Never give up, be patient, be kind to yourself and others, and remember, if it's broken, fix it, and if you can't fix it, where does it go? In the bin!

I leave you the way I met you, with a poem I wrote about the ego (the tiger), our true essence (the I) and the illusion of life (the dream).

I hope you like it.

The Tiger, The I, The Dream

The ego, a roaring tiger who protects the worldly self:
Extant so the I can experience the wondrous dream of life.
When the I observed the tiger, its ferocity was no more,
Its roar disappeared completely:
And a friend not foe was born.

The tiger roars each day you see,
and the I did turn and say:
You're a thought, a feeling, a memory,
now put those teeth away.

You're a shadow born of mind, dear friend:
and I need no protection.
There is eternal light in me,
no harm will come my direction.

Don't growl and snarl and roar, dear friend:
You're merely my reflection,
Look inward, know thyself, I say:
You'll find here deep affection.

Head back into your cage once more,
Your teeth are not so sharp,
You're only roaring at illusions:
Of a wakened, dreamlike part.

The Tiger, The I, The Dream.

Sat Nam,
Steve

Printed in Great Britain
by Amazon

25925614R00096